Cambridge Elements

Elements in Magic
edited by
William Pooley
University of Bristol

THE ELIXIR

A Posthumanist Approach to Alchemy in Akbarian Sufism and Islam

Dunja Rašić
Tampere University
and
Muhyiddin Ibn Arabi Society

CAMBRIDGE
UNIVERSITY PRESS

CAMBRIDGE
UNIVERSITY PRESS

Shaftesbury Road, Cambridge CB2 8EA, United Kingdom

One Liberty Plaza, 20th Floor, New York, NY 10006, USA

477 Williamstown Road, Port Melbourne, VIC 3207, Australia

314–321, 3rd Floor, Plot 3, Splendor Forum, Jasola District Centre, New Delhi – 110025, India

103 Penang Road, #05–06/07, Visioncrest Commercial, Singapore 238467

Cambridge University Press is part of Cambridge University Press & Assessment, a department of the University of Cambridge.

We share the University's mission to contribute to society through the pursuit of education, learning and research at the highest international levels of excellence.

www.cambridge.org
Information on this title: www.cambridge.org/9781009777018

DOI: 10.1017/9781009777032

When citing this work, please include a reference to the DOI 10.1017/9781009777032

First published 2025

A catalogue record for this publication is available from the British Library

A Cataloging-in-Publication data record for this Element is available from the Library of Congress

ISBN 978-1-009-77740-7 Hardback
ISBN 978-1-009-77701-8 Paperback
ISSN 2732-4087 (online)
ISSN 2732-4079 (print)

The Elixir

A Posthumanist Approach to Alchemy in Akbarian Sufism and Islam

Elements in Magic

DOI: 10.1017/9781009777032
First published online: December 2025

Dunja Rašić
Tampere University
and
Muhyiddin Ibn Arabi Society

Author for correspondence: Dunja Rašić, rasic@bgsmcs.fu-berlin.de

Abstract: Step outside the laboratory and into the world of nature. The books on canon law can be left behind as well, for Ibn ʿArabī (d. 1240) believed there is one Sharia for humans and another for minerals. This Element rethinks what it means to be an alchemist and Muslim by shifting its focus to the religious practices of sentient minerals, as described in Ibn ʿArabī's oeuvre and the Qur'an. Common stones and metals perform their spiritual feats with a single goal in mind: to gain proximity to the divine by turning themselves into gold. Alchemists sought to facilitate this process through elixirs and sorcery. Setting allegories and metaphors aside, this Element examines the ontological principles governing the struggles of iron to become gold and the human strivings to better the world of nature.

Keywords: Ibn ʿArabi, alchemy, posthumanism, magic, minerals

ISBNs: 9781009777407 (HB), 9781009777018 (PB), 9781009777032 (OC)
ISSNs: 2732-4087 (online), 2732-4079 (print)

Contents

1 Introduction 1

2 Anything but Magic! 4

3 A Posthumanist Approach 11

4 Seek Knowledge, Even as Far as China! 16

5 The Roots of Corruption 30

6 Mineral Magic: (Extra)ordinary Transmutations 47

7 The Alchemy of Red Sulphur 51

8 In Conclusion 56

Bibliography 61

1 Introduction

Descendants of Ḥātim al-Ṭā'iyy, the warrior-poet of Shammar, were reputed for chivalry, generosity and shrewdness. Their reputation spread to Europe in 1706, through the tales of *One Thousand and One Nights*. None born of the Ṭā'iyy line has attained the lasting fame of Muḥyī al-Dīn Ibn ʿArabī to date. A scion of the Yemenite branch of the Ṭā'iyy tribe, Ibn ʿArabī was born in Murcia in 1165. He was the direct descendant of the first Arab dignitaries (*buyūtāt*) to settle in the Iberian Peninsula at the outset of Ṭāriq b. Ziyād's war against the Visigoths (711–719). His father ʿAlī secured a post at the Almohad court in Seville for himself and Ibn ʿArabī was expected to follow in his footsteps. Disregarding the opposition of his family, he embarked on the Sufi path instead. He travelled far and wide in search of knowledge – across the Maghreb, Egypt, Hejaz, Anatolia and the Levant. When death found him in Damascus in 1240, he had the following couplet ready to be engraved at the entrance of his mausoleum:

> In every age there is one after whom it is named;
> for the remaining ages I am that one!

Stephen Hirtenstein, who first translated Ibn ʿArabī's epitaph into English, did not think it an exaggeration.[1] Ibn ʿArabī remains a defining voice in philosophical and theological discourses eight centuries after his death. Today, the popularity of his writings is at an all-time high,[2] with Mark Sedgwick suggesting that he gradually came to epitomize Sufism in the West.[3] Equally famous are Ibn ʿArabī's contributions to jurisprudence, poetry and the hermeneutics of the Qur'an. He is seldom regarded as an alchemist, however. Ibn ʿArabī's quest for red sulphur (*al-kibrīt al-aḥmar*), which is a legendary substance that can turn common stones and metals into gold, escaped academic scrutiny at large. The same could be said about alchemical practices in Muslim cultures and societies between the tenth and the fifteenth century.[4] This is where my Element steps in, to map out a portion of this terra incognita.

---

[1] Ibn ʿArabī's epitaph was quoted according to Hirtenstein, *The Unlimited Mercifier*, p. 6. Further biographical information on Ibn ʿArabi can be found in Claude Addas's seminal work on the topic, Quest for the Red Sulphur: The Life of Ibn ʿArabī.

[2] Abdel-hadi, *Ibn ʿArabī's Religious Pluralism*, p. i.

[3] Sedgwick, 'Ibn ʿArabi and the Contemporary West', p. 389.

[4] In 2016, Regula Forster dismissed prior scholarship on Arabo-Islamic alchemy as 'rudimentary' at best. 'Research was essentially limited to the early period, i.e. the time up to the 10th century, and more recently to the Ottoman alchemy and its interaction with Paracelsian iatrochemistry. Thus, we lack work on the period in-between,' she said. Forster, 'Zwischen Religion und Alchemie', p. 11. Nine years later, we lack it still.

Alchemy, broadly defined, refers to the art of turning common stones and metals into gold. This Element will examine how the royal art was perceived in Akbarian circles during the mid thirteenth century, in Ibn ʿArabī's lifetime.[5] It builds and expands on the Qur'anic notion of minerals as sentient beings, whom God endowed with the ability to think, speak and feel. Ibn ʿArabī espoused the same views as the Qur'an, which led him to explore religious beliefs and practices of common stones and metals. Minerals were recognized as pious Muslims and alchemists in Ibn ʿArabī's works. He was convinced that iron could turn itself into gold without human interference. Inspired by Ibn ʿArabī, my Element adopts an innovative posthumanist approach to Arabo-Islamic alchemy, inviting the reader to rethink what it means to practise alchemy *and* Islam from the point of view of a mineral. The contribution of this Element to knowledge advancement is threefold: 1) it will introduce the reader to the ontological principles governing the transformation of common stones and metals into gold that Ibn ʿArabī described; 2) it will examine the sources of knowledge, power and authority in Arabo-Islamic alchemy between the ninth and the thirteenth centuries which allow for the posthumanist approach to alchemy; and 3) it will challenge the paradigm of reducing Ibn ʿArabī's alchemical oeuvre to allegories and metaphors for the spiritual ascension of humans, which is prevalent in contemporary scholarship. In short, my Element will bring overlooked elements of Ibn ʿArabī's writings on the kingdom of minerals to the forefront, offering a new understanding of what it means to be a Muslim, an alchemist and a mineral specimen in the sentient cosmos that Ibn ʿArabī envisioned. The ultimate goal is to enrich global perspectives on alchemy and foster intercultural engagement through an exploration of Ibn ʿArabī's teachings.

The alchemical writings of Muḥyī al-Dīn Ibn ʿArabī cannot be studied apart from his views on magic (this is yet another terra incognita to be mapped out in this Element). Ibn ʿArabī taught that the occult properties of stones, plants and letters are the roots of jinn magic (*sīmiyāʾ*), which is a blameworthy knowledge as far as Sharia is concerned.[6] Jinn are the fire spirits described in the Qur'an, whimsical and brash. These spirits know all about magic and nothing about morals. Sufi practices, by contrast, are

[5] A note on terminology: Ibn ʿArabī has been referred to as *shaykh al-akbar*, the Greatest Shaykh, as of the thirteenth century. His followers thus came to be known as 'Akbarians'. A comprehensive analysis of Ibn ʿArabī's sobriquets and the titles he held can be found in Hirtenstein, 'Names and Titles of Ibn [al-]ʿArabī', pp. 109–131.

[6] Ibn ʿArabī, *al-Futūḥāt al-Makkiyya*, vol. 1, pp. 273–274. Henceforth: FM.I: 273–274.

rooted in adherence to Sharia and proper moral conduct.[7] Students and successors of Ibn ʿArabī showed little incentive to rival the jinn working their magic with precious stones and metals. Magic was generally looked down upon among Sufis and there are lines of text echoing this sentiment in Ibn ʿArabī's books as well. However, Ibn ʿArabī also taught that dabbling in sorcery (*siḥr*) can be praiseworthy at times.[8] 'There are as many definitions of magic and divination as there are people writing on the subject', Emilie Savage-Smith observed.[9] Ibn ʿArabī adopted a broad definition in his works, encompassing (almost) every successful intervention performed by a contingent life form aiming to suspend the laws of nature and break the conventional order of things (*kharq al-ʿāda*).[10] Most interventions he described center around arcane properties of the letters of the Arabic alphabet. Observing skies and horoscopes and working with the forces of nature and the ninety-nine names of God were among the alternative methods he suggested.[11] Ibn ʿArabī made no distinction between jinn magic and sorcery, and he used the word 'siḥr' (sorcery) as a synonym for 'sīmiyā'' (magic).[12] Thaumaturges' race was of no importance to him: what makes a sorcerer is their ability to defy the laws of nature and bend the world to their will. The coveted ability to turn iron into gold meets this criterion. A closer examination of the premises leading to this assertion might be warranted, however, given that alchemy tends to be described as 'natural philosophy' and a 'predecessor of chemistry',[13] rather than 'magic'. This is the topic for the section to come (Section 2).

Scholars have long recognized the dual nature of alchemy encompassing both theory and practice.[14] Ibn ʿArabī himself placed greater value on

[7] This interpretation draws from Ibn ʿArabī's definition of Sufism (*taṣawwuf*), which can be consulted at FM.II: 128.

[8] FM.II: 135.

[9] Savage-Smith (ed.), *Magic and Divination in Early Islam*, p. xiii.

[10] FM.II: 135. Note that at no point did Ibn ʿArabī equate direct divine interventions with sorcery. He referred to indirect divine interventions – e.g. when God empowers His prophets to act in His name – as '*muʿjizāt*'. The latter were only ever performed when the authority of a certain prophet was challenged, and laymen were incapable of replicating them (which is not the case with alchemy). FM.I: 235–236; FM.II: 374.

[11] FM.II: 371.

[12] For instance, see FM.II: 135.

[13] For instance, see Ulmann, *Die Natur*, pp. 10–11 and Forster, 'Arabic Alchemy', pp. 270–271. The word 'magic' is rarely featured in contemporary definitions of alchemy. Ibn ʿArabī's works were penned 800 years ago, however, when smiths were traditionally regarded as thaumaturges. 'Because of their ability to control forces of transformation and destruction, metalworkers often had important role in society and were called to perform magic,' Chris Gosden observed. See Gosden, *The History of Magic*, p. 304.

[14] Alchemical practices, Michela Pereira noted, 'so much resembled well-established craftsmen's labor (metal melting, working on minerals, glassmaking) that for a long period, the

knowing how gold is brought into existence – whether through divine agency or human intervention – than on the power required to execute alchemical transmutations. Nonetheless, he maintained that mastery of alchemy equals theory and practice combined.[15] The theoretical knowledge he had in mind extends beyond the transformation of divine spirit into prime matter, stones and metals (a subject outlined in Section 5). Permanent alchemical transmutations cannot be undertaken without expertise in metallurgy and mineralogy, prompting alchemists to seek this knowledge as far as Egypt (Ibn ᶜArabī's reflections on the kingdom of minerals and the origins of alchemy will be examined in Sections 3 and 4). An overview of theories expounding the nature and origins of red sulphur (Section 7) will be accompanied by Ibn ᶜArabī's instructions on how to refine coarse matter so as to make it resemble the divine spirit in perfection (Section 6). The concluding section of the Element pivots on Ibn ᶜArabī's notion of alchemy as an affront to God and a crime against humankind, while also delineating the rare circumstances under which the righteous (*ṣāliḥūn*) may be permitted to practise it.

2 Anything but Magic!

When Sean McLoughlin described the alchemical transmutations Ibn ᶜArabī performed as 'a work that is contrary to nature', he did so under the assumption that alchemists intervene to prevent nature from taking its course. McLoughlin saw their interventions as 'the act of strife, a supernatural resonance, and a liberation is born from bonds that normally compel the life process'.[16] But here is the catch: Ibn ᶜArabī shared Aristotle's view that all things in existence strive for perfection and the prophet Muhammad exemplified the perfect human being in his works. Buraq, the celestial steed that carried Muhammad to the seventh heaven, is the pinnacle of animal perfection. Ibn ᶜArabī furthermore taught that the *wāqwāq* tree epitomizes the perfection of fauna. Within every class of existence, Ibn ᶜArabī noted, there is a singular perfect exemplar, and that distinction belongs to gold among minerals.[17] Aztec royalty preferred quetzal feathers to gold and King Petar I of Serbia felt that a crown made of a bronze cannon handle was best suited for the ruler of a warrior nation. Such examples are rare,

---

place of alchemy in the divisio disciplinarum wavered between the mechanical and the liberal arts'. Pereira, 'Alchemy and the Use of Vernacular Languages in the Late Middle Ages', pp. 336–337.

[15] FM.II: 460–461.

[16] McLoughlin, 'Preliminary Notes on Ibn Arabi and Alchemy', p. 3.

[17] FM.III: 347. See also FM.II: 647.

however. Most sovereigns crowned themselves with gold and King Petar's subjects, displeased by his unconventional choice (which they attributed to excessive frugality), made sure his crown was gold-coated at least. There is near universal admiration for gold among mankind and Ibn ʿArabī suspected that the rebel-sorcerer Samiri consciously sought to exploit it to lure people to idolatry: 'Before their eyes he fashioned a gold calf from their jewelry, knowing that the hearts of people are attached to their wealth. And so, when he invited them to worship the calf, they rushed to do so.'[18] People who are attached to their wealth, Ibn ʿArabī said, happily turn to murder, and they would not hesitate to kill God himself if they came to suspect Him of hindering their alchemical pursuits. Alchemists dare not practise their art openly, in fear of this ilk.[19] On his side, Ibn ʿArabī maintained that no true alchemist is enamored with wealth. He valued gold nonetheless 'as a symbol of the pinnacle stages of spiritual ascension and rank. Gold possesses the quality of perfect balance, and it is the most noble of metals,' he said.[20] Were a mineral to be left to its own devices, it would take around 36,000 years for it to reach the perfection of gold.[21] This is a lengthy process to be sure, but it does not violate the laws of nature (as opposed to sorcery).

Supernatural impacts of sorcery were referred to as miracles by Ibn ʿArabī. There is a curious statement in Ibn ʿArabī's book *al-Futūḥāt* indicating that a spiritual feat must be one of a kind to be classified as 'kharq al-ʿāda', which is the term Ibn ʿArabī used as a synonym for sorcery and the breaking of conventional order of things. 'The breach happens only once and repetition signals convention,' he said.[22] Thus, one could argue that repeated alchemical transmutations cannot be regarded as sorcery – although Ibn ʿArabī did not apply this standard to the spiritual feats of his acquaintances, who could make themselves immune to fire and conjure living beings and objects out of thin air repeatedly. In other words, a certain lack of originality was not always a detriment for a spiritual feat to be seen as a breaking of the conventional order of things, as far as Ibn ʿArabī was concerned.[23] An alchemical transmutation could be deemed miraculous even if Ibn ʿArabī's standards were to be applied

18 FM.I: 574.

19 FM.II: 420–421. As Section 8 will demonstrate, Ibn ʿArabī believed that God obstructs most alchemical transmutations.

20 Ibn ʿArabī, *Sharh tarjumān al-ashwāq*, p. 165.

21 FM.I: 592–593.

22 FM.II: 372.

23 For instance, see FM.II: 370–371.

strictly – not because it *happened*, but because of the swift conclusion of synthetic transmutations in a controlled environment. For instance, some of the most elaborate transmutations that al-Rāzī (d. 925) described take up to forty days to complete – which is miraculously short when compared to the average duration of natural transmutations (36,000 years according to Ibn ʿArabī).[24] Another factor to be considered is that climate change and weather conditions can get in the way of natural transmutations. As a result, most minerals will never turn into gold outside of the laboratory.[25] An alchemist facilitating the transmutation of iron into gold could thus be regarded as a thaumaturge for bringing the whole process to the optimal conclusion swiftly.

Some alchemists, Ibn ʿArabī said, also work on creating precious stones: emeralds, rubies, sapphires and the like. Describing alchemy as 'natural philosophy' would not be erroneous per se since permanent transmutations require an in-depth knowledge of mineralogy, prime matter and climatology (see Sections 4 and 5), and since Ibn ʿArabī broadly defined philosophy as the love of wisdom (*ḥubb al-ḥikma*).[26] That being said, Ibn ʿArabī explicitly referred to alchemical transmutations as '*kharq al-ʿāda*, which constitutes a miraculous breach of the laws of nature' in *al-Futūḥāt*.[27] Thus, he implicitly identified alchemy with sorcery. 'Karamāt' is another term Ibn ʿArabī used to describe alchemical transmutations and the knowledge required to undertake them.[28] Here it ought to be noted that 'karamāt' was the established term for saintly miracles among Sufis. The word 'sorcery' (*siḥr*) was reserved for the accomplishments of a competing shaykh instead. Indignantly, Sufi shaykhs protested against the impertinence of the ulama who counted them among sorcerers, the friends of the Devil (*awliyāʾ al-shayṭān*). The gist of their argument Ibn ʿArabī repeated is that God's friends can learn from Him directly. Sorcerers must rely on other humans, books and

[24] Marlow Taylor (trans.), *The Alchemy of al-Razi*, pp. 124–277. Elias Ashmole (d. 1692) shared this view as well. An alchemist merely speeds natural processes up, he said. Linden, *The Alchemy Reader*, pp. 14–15.

[25] FM.I: 592–593. This is not to say that nature is hostile to minerals: lightning, gusts of wind, the warmth of the Sun and clouds all seek to purify Earth and its inhabitants. FM.I: 121–122. However, benevolent forces of nature do not always have a positive effect on the spiritual growth of minerals. More often than not, climate and weather will hinder the transformation of iron into gold in nature.

[26] FM.II: 532. Alchemists were generally referred to as *ḥukamāʾ* in the early modern and medieval religious works and literature in Arabic. Hassan, *Studies in al-Kimiyaʾ*, p. 7.

[27] FM.II 460–461.

[28] FM.II: 420–421.

jinn to deduce a method to turn the world upside down.[29] Ibn ʿArabī was recognized as a recipient of divine knowledge since he was around fifteen years of age, and his fame has grown since. So when Ibn Khaldūn (d. 1406) levelled accusations of sorcery against him, a chorus of defenders swiftly emerged.[30] The provocative statements Ibn ʿArabī made complicated the efforts to vindicate him completely. Among other things, he noted that 'although God's friends do not label what they do as "sorcery", opting for the term "karamāt" instead, their feats causing the conventional order of things to break align precisely with the definition of sorcery by religious scholars'.[31] Ibn ʿArabī spoke candidly about the spiritual feats he *himself* had performed (e.g. chasing away the angel of death to save the lives of his friends) and he made some of his talismans available to general public. This caused no small embarrassment to his supporters,[32] prompting them to take drastic measures at times.

Not all witches were burned out of history. This was the fate befitting social outcasts, widows and the poor. Fāṭima bt. al-Muthannā, who was the spiritual mother of Ibn ʿArabī, fit the criteria. When Fāṭima was accused of sorcery, stones rained down on her.[33] There are other ways to erase witchcraft from cultural history than exposing books and bodies to fire, however, and hatred was not the single driving force behind the erasure. Ibn ʿArabī's students in particular did not wish to destroy but to protect their shaykh. Some of the talismans he made available in his holographs thus came to be removed from *every* subsequent edition of the text,[34] and his writings on celestial magic and demonology have been systematically ignored. Contemporary scholars adopted a similar approach. 'It is peculiar, to say the least, that a vast and complicated domain of religious and intellectual activity … should have been ignored by the academy as if it did not exist – or threated as if it *should* not exist,' Hanegraaff said with regard to Western esotericism.[35] Diane Purkiss went

[29] See FM.I: 263, FM.II: 360–370, 461. See also Ibn ʿArabī, K. al-Mīm (MS Veliyuddin 1759), ff.1.

[30] Ibn Khaldūn, *al-Muqaddima*, vol. 3, pp. 171–172.

[31] FM.II: 135. A hairsplitting analysis of the subtle differences Ibn ʿArabī made between *siḥr* and *karāmāt* at times can be found at Rašić, 'Fāṭima, the Righteous Sorceress', pp. 364–381.

[32] Consult Ruspoli, *Le Livre des théophanies d'Ibn Arabî*, p. 108, on the reception of Ibn ʿArabī's talismans among his followers. On death-thwarting rites in Akbarian Sufism and Islam, see Rašić, *Azrael*.

[33] FM.I: 274; Ibn ʿArabī, *Sufis of Andalusia*, pp. 143–146.

[34] Further information on one such talisman can be found at Rašić, 'Summoned Letters, Disjointed Letters and the Talisman of Ibn ʿArabī', pp. 1–15.

[35] Hanegraaf, *Western Esotericism*, p. 2.

further, criticizing her colleagues for 'explaining witch-beliefs away'.[36] Alison Roberts exemplified these tendencies in her reading of Ibn ʿArabī's alchemy of red sulphur as a metaphor for human development – 'not as an occult, magical science in contradistinction to the Sufi ascetic, mystical path, nor as the forerunner of chemistry'.[37] Claude Addas likewise stressed that red sulphur 'is often used in Sufi vocabulary as a metaphor indicating the excellence of the spiritual level attained by a saint'.[38] Gold was another prominent symbol of spiritual excellence in Ibn ʿArabī's works, Titus Burckhardt quipped.[39] Therefore, although Ibn ʿArabī's books contain references to alchemy, 'it is an alchemy that is not concerned with transforming base metals into gold, except in a symbolic sense'.[40] Abū Bakr b. Bishrūn, who studied alchemy under Maslama al-Majrīṭī (d. 1007), the author of *Picatrix*, made a similar attempt to exonerate both his teacher and himself. Their detractors remained unmollified, however, with Ibn Khaldūn claiming that the frequent use of symbols and metaphors in alchemical treatises warranted their classification as sorcery. Sternly, he judged Ibn ʿArabī and Ibn Bishrūn guilty of this crime.

> One can see how alchemists turn every expression into secret hints and puzzles, scarcely to be explained or understood. This is proof of the fact that alchemy is not a natural science. The truth with regard to alchemy, which is to be believed and which is supported by actual fact, is that alchemy is one of the ways in which the spiritual souls exercise influence and are active in the world of nature. It may belong among the miraculous acts of divine grace (*karāmāt*), if the souls are good. Or it may be a kind of sorcery if the souls are bad and wicked.[41]

Not only were the attempts to exonerate Ibn ʿArabī by restricting his thought to metaphor inefficient – but they also convey only part of the truth. Now, to be clear: alchemical discourse requires the reader to wield

[36] Purkiss, *The Witch in History*, p. 61.

[37] Roberts, 'Rectifying the Pharaoh', p. 2.

[38] Addas, *The Quest for the Red Sulphur*, p. 112. This is not to imply that Addas was unfamiliar with Ibn ʿArabī's views on red sulphur. Her research was consciously restricted to metaphors.

[39] Burckhardt, *Alchemy*, p. 126. No references were provided by Burckhardt to back up his assertion. Yet this does not negate the validity of his insight. Moving beyond the customary dismissal of 'competing' interpretations on technicalities in academia, I am offering the missing reference here to make a point: FM.I: 10.

[40] See Jaffray's commentary and translation of *K. al- al-Isrāʾ* in Ibn ʿArabī, *The Secrets of Voyaging*, pp. 226–227.

[41] Ibn Khaldūn, *al-Muqaddima*, vol. 3, p. 247. Cf. Anawati, 'Arabic Alchemy', p. 880. It was previously demonstrated that Ibn ʿArabī, unlike Ibn Khaldūn, did not always make a distinction between *siḥr* and *karāmāt* himself.

metaphor like a key, unlocking hidden layers of meaning. A skeleton key of a sort was supplanted by Abū al-Qāsim al-Irāqī (d. 1260), a self-professed alchemist from Baghdad. Al-Irāqī identified three types of statements in the writings of colleagues:

1. Plain speech devoid of allegories
2. Broad statements that could be used as allegories, such as: 'Humans are rational animals.'
3. Phrases of necessary associations, such as: 'He is brave like a lion.'

Alchemical manuals, al-Irāqī said, are mostly comprised of statements of the third type. This is especially the case with the texts discussing the properties of precious stones and metals. For instance, if an alchemist were to refer to quicksilver as 'eastern mercury', this does not necessarily mean it hails from a region east of Egypt, but rather that it was extracted from stones whose nature is hot and dry – much like the lands of the East. 'Heaven' is a metaphor for volatile substances in alchemical manuals, stable substances are referred to as 'earth', 'marriage' is the term used for mixing substances together – the list goes on. Al-Irāqī felt confident that the full list he disclosed would render alchemical manuscripts accessible to a broader audience. A little gratitude toward the one who provided access to arcane knowledge others have kept for themselves might be in order, he said.[42] Al-Irāqī recognized his colleagues for the secretive cabal they were; they withheld valuable information even from their closest friends and disciples until shortly before death.[43] Pseudo-Zosimos was more generous than most, supplanting al-Irāqī's list with explanation that 'sulphur' is a metaphor for combustible substances. Red sulphur, which is the philosopher's stone, could be consequently described as a combustible substance, solid of form (its form being the reason why alchemists refer to it as 'stone').[44] Ibn ᶜArabī, who was fond of metaphors himself, referred to prophets as 'gryphons'. He also used 'red sulphur' as a metaphor for a perfect human being *at times.* Claude Addas and Alison Roberts rightly

---

42 al-Irāqī, *Book of Knowledge*, pp. 55–57.

43 For instance, see Haq, *Names, Natures and Things*, p. 36; Marlow Taylor, *The Alchemy of al-Razi*, pp. 99–100 and Linden, *The Alchemy Reader*, pp. 73–80.

44 Zosimos, *Muṣḥaf al-ṣuwar*, pp. 175–176. Greek alchemist Zosimos of Panopolis died circa AD 300. However, Benjamin Hallum convincingly argued that the book *Muṣḥaf al-ṣuwar,* which is traditionally attributed to Zosimos, was penned by an anonymous Arab alchemist in the Middle Ages. Zosimos, *Muṣḥaf al-ṣuwar*, pp. 117–118. Medieval alchemists often attributed their works to famous figures such as Plato, Aristotle, Pythagoras, Hermes Trismegistos and Cleopatra. Concrete examples can be found in Hassan, *Studies in al-Kimiya'*, p. 9.

underscored this point. The mistake would be to think that metaphor is all there is to it, however. William Newman said:

> In reading historians of chemistry, one sometimes encounters the claim that mercury and sulphur, the supposed components of [all] metals, were believed by alchemists to be 'metaphysical', 'spiritual' or 'ideal' entities, in contrast to the material constituents of things envisioned by the eighteenth-century chemistry. According to this view, alchemists generally acknowledged that their principles were incapable of being handled or observed, as they were too pure and 'high' to be isolated by means attainable in a workshop or laboratory. The origin of these claims is obscure, but they are severely undercut by several considerations. First, it is not clear what is meant by terms like 'metaphysical,' 'spiritual,' or 'ideal.' What I want to suggest is that the sulphur and mercury of High Medieval alchemy were usually the material substances that share those names on the modern periodic table: yet unlike our modern elements, the medieval principles were often viewed in the same light as impure ores and other minerals that had to be refined before use.[45]

Newman's reflections on contemporary readings of Arabo-Latin alchemical texts bear relevance to Ibn ᶜArabī's oeuvre and the broader debate on the exoteric (*ẓāhir*) and esoteric (*bāṭin*) dimension of religious literature in Islam. Ibn ᶜArabī acknowledged both these dimensions in his works and he described the text of the Qur'an in particular as an ocean without shore. Mining the depths of its esoteric meanings is a risky venture. The safety of knowledge, Ibn ᶜArabī advised, lies in adhering to the literal meaning of the text.[46] His readers disregarded the shaykh's advice at times, favouring every conceivable interpretation of his writings on red sulphur except the literal one. Perhaps it was easier for them to accept and rationalize the possibility of inner spiritual transformation – that a small human could become *al-insān al-kāmil*, the Perfect Human and God's viceregent on Earth – than to seriously entertain the prospect of turning iron into gold. Another thing to be considered is that Sufism is traditionally identified with renunciation of the visible world, which Ibn ᶜArabī compared to 'a stinking, dried up corpse'.[47] This posed a dilemma for his followers, who struggled to reconcile the shaykh's willingness to discuss, let alone perform, operations aimed at creating gold *metal*. The central goal of this Element is to expound Ibn ᶜArabī's methods and motives behind the alchemical transmutations he performed.

[45] Newman, 'Mercury and Sulphur', pp. 327–328.
[46] FM.II: 119.
[47] Ibn ᶜArabī, *Divine Governance of the Human Kingdom*, p. 66.

3 A Posthumanist Approach

My Element will not dwell on spiritual psychology at length. Rather, it centres around the art of cultivating gold metal (*ṣanʿat zirāʿat al-dhahab*), which Ibn ʿArabī identified with sorcery at times. If some regard this as the lowest form of alchemy, so be it.[48] The principal body of Ibn ʿArabī's writings on the topic is preserved in the following treatises:

- *al-Futūḥāt al-Makkiyya* (*The Meccan Revelations*)
- *K. Manzil al-manāzil* (*The Station of Stations*)
- *K. Mashāhid al-asrār al-qudsiyya* (*Contemplations of the Holy Mysteries*)
- *K. al-Tadbīrāt al-ilāhiyya* (*Divine Governance of the Human Kingdom*)
- *K. al-Quṭb wal-imāmayn* (*Treatise on the Pole and Two Imams*)
- *Mawāqiʿ al-nujūm* (*The Twilight of the Stars*)
- *Risāla al-Anwār* (*Epistle of Lights*)
- *ʿUqlat al-mustawfiz* (*The Bridle of the Restless*)

Prior scholarship has focused on chapter 167 of *al-Futūḥāt* for the most part. This is hardly surprising since *al-Futūḥāt* is regarded as Ibn ʿArabī's magnum opus and masterpiece. The title of chapter 167, 'On the Spiritual Knowledge of the Alchemy of Happiness' (*fī maʿrifa kīmiyāʿ al-saʿāda*), alludes to Ibn ʿArabī's understanding of alchemy as the knowledge of the elixir (*al-ʿilm bil-iksīr*) that will bring everlasting happiness to God's creation. The roots of this happiness are spiritual perfection and bodily health, which are exemplified by gold.[49] When Stephen Hirtenstein translated chapter 167 of *al-Futūḥāt* into English, he opted for the title 'The Alchemy of *Human* Happiness'. It was a conscious decision Hirtenstein made to underline Ibn ʿArabī's concern for the well-being of humans.

Ibn ʿArabī recognized that humans are but one of the species God created nonetheless; they share the world of nature with the jinn-folk, plants and animals. Now, imagine Earth surrounded by celestial spheres. A drawing based on Ibn ʿArabī's artwork can be found below (Figure 1). The shaykh referred to spheres above Earth as the Greater Kingdom (*al-mulk al-akbar*) and he divided earthly realms into the kingdoms of humans, minerals, plants and animals. The collaborative survival of living beings, Anna Tsing noted, necessitates cross-species cooperation. Philosophers in the West have refused to acknowledge this reality since the Age of Enlightenment, she said. And so Tsing called for men and women from around the world,

[48] For instance, see Hamarneh, 'Arabic-Islamic Alchemy', p. 74, 84. Cf. Flequer, 'The Science of Letters', p. 12.

[49] FM.II: 270–271.

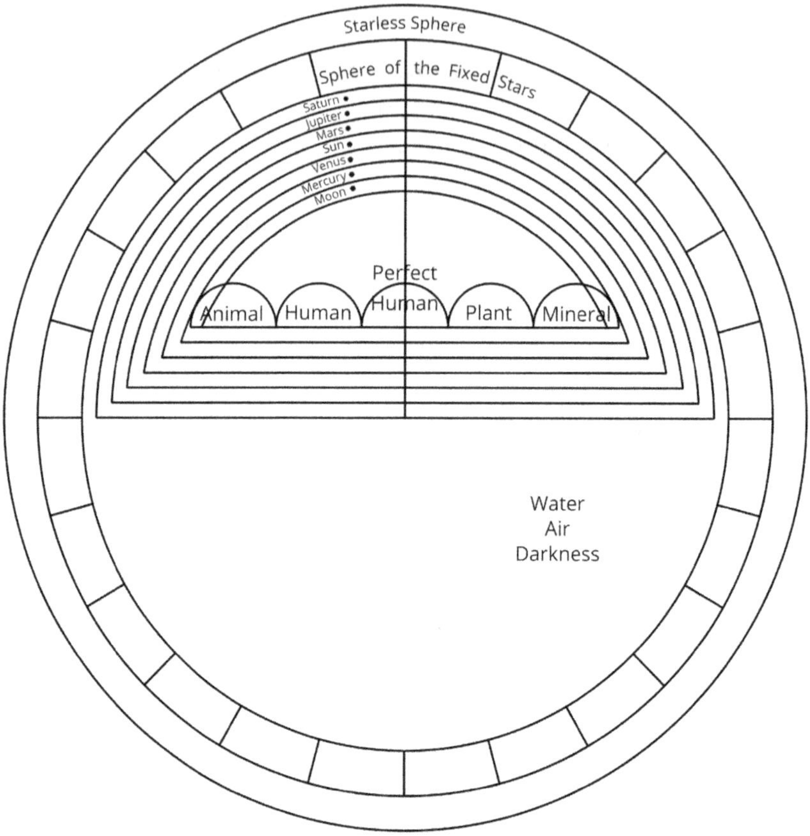

Figure 1 Celestial spheres. Drawing by the author based on Ibn ʿArabī's *al-Futūḥāt al-Makkiyya* (MS YAZMA ff. 92. Istanbul: Museum of Turkish and Islamic Arts, 636 AH).

the uncivilized, to challenge 'the moral intentionality of Man's Christian masculinity, which separates Man from Nature'.[50] The riotous voice of Jakob von Uexküll likewise maintained that perception, communications and purposeful behaviour of nonhumans must be taken into account for any biology to be worthy of its name. The willingness to do so, von Uexküll said, commences the transmutation of a biologist into metaphysician, 'who looks for effective factors behind the physical world'.[51] Von Uexküll and Tsing are both recognized for their contribution to posthumanist studies, which are often conflated with ontology, ecohumanism, speculative realism and metaphysics. This is hardly surprising,

[50] Tsing, *The Mushroom at the End of the World*, pp. vii–viii.
[51] Von Uexküll, *A Foray into the Worlds of Animals and Humans*, p. 159.

given that 'posthumanism' is the established term for philosophies centring around nonhuman life forms. Cary Wolfe tracked the origins of posthumanism back to the 1960s and defined it as 'every philosophical work that takes the moral status of nonhuman animals seriously'.[52] Caution was ever the defining factor limiting posthumanist inquiries to companion animals and mammals. 'I have chosen [to focus on] bats instead of wasps or flounders', Nagel said, 'because if one travels too far down the phylogenetic tree, people gradually shed their faith that there is experience there at all.'[53] Few had von Uexküll's daring to try to envision the lived experience of scallops, ticks and molluscs. Seven hundred years prior, Ibn ʿArabī turned his attention to minerals.

A posthumanist approach to alchemy means examining transmutations from the vantage point of living, breathing representatives of the mineral kingdom. Humans must be content with a peripheral role in this Element centring around minerals attempting to get closer to God. Upon reaching their goal, the corporeal form of minerals turns into gold. Ontological, cosmological and metaphysical principles governing alchemical transmutations will be examined in Sections 6 and 7, respectively. It is, however, necessary to pinpoint what constitutes a mineral life form before we proceed. We will begin by listing the recognized inhabitants of the kingdom of minerals in Ibn ʿArabī's works: pearls and corals, gemstones such as emeralds, rubies and sapphires, phosphorus, crystals such as spinel, and metals such as iron, copper, silver and gold. The soil itself also belongs to this kingdom.[54] Mineral bodies, all of them, are comprised of fire, water, air and earth. The same holds true for every inhabitant of the world of nature. Were it otherwise, Ibn ʿArabī said, the food chain would collapse. Living beings can only consume things that are similar to them in nature: this is what Ibn ʿArabī believed. A plant could not get nourishment from the soil if it were not for the fact that both the plant and the soil are made of the four elements. Ibn ʿArabī stopped short of revealing what kind of nourishment God provides for minerals and whether the preferred diet of sapphires is different to that of iron. He was, however, adamant that minerals must eat *and* breathe to live.[55] The same holds true for every living being He created.

Here it should be noted that Ibn ʿArabī compared stones to carcasses at times – and he also said that minerals correspond to those aspects

[52] Wolfe, *What Is Posthumanism?*, p. 62.
[53] Nagel, 'What Is It Like to Be a Bat?', p. 438.
[54] FM.I: 598. See also Bosnevi, *Marātib al-wujūd*, p. 157.
[55] FM.I: 95–96; FM.IV: 219, 323.

of human nature that were devoid of sensation and awareness (*mā lā yaḥusu*).[56] These were but figures of speech, however. In chapter 365 of *al-Futūḥāt* he explained that the whole world is alive and conscious. 'One cannot divide [things] of the universe into living and inanimate things. We believe that the universe is alive in its totality,' Ibn ʿArabī said.[57] He was personally convinced that every mineral had a soul akin to the vegetable soul of humans (*al-nafs al-nabātiyya*).[58] The mineral soul is capable of learning since it is imbued with divine light.[59] Ibn ʿArabī did not approve of his contemporaries claiming that minerals lack intelligence. Stones and metals would be incapable of worshipping God if that were the case.[60] Now, Wittgenstein and Descartes questioned the intelligence of animals on the grounds they cannot speak. Since the ability to think is rooted in language, Descartes claimed, an animal can only 'react' but never respond consciously when challenged.[61] If a lion could talk, Wittgenstein said, we could not understand him – and he furthermore argued that 'to imagine a language is to imagine a form of life'.[62] Daniel Dennett, who was critical of posthumanist studies, agreed that lions cannot communicate with humans. If we were to find a lion that *could* speak, Dennett said, this would be nothing short of a miracle. And because this lion would be one of a kind, 'insights and information received from it would be practically worthless and couldn't be relied upon to learn anything about the inner workings of a lion pride – and no other lion whatsoever'.[63] The question of whether minerals can speak was not addressed by Descartes, Wittgenstein and/or Dennett. No posthumanist study I know of explored this possibility in earnest – and the same goes for the anonymous thirteenth-century scholars Ibn ʿArabī criticized.

56 'Mineral' components of the human body include teeth and nails. See FM.I: 55, 121, 136 and FM.II: 78, 687.

57 FM.III: 324. Note that Ibn ʿArabī did not think that life force was an essential attribute of the body. He rather described it as an accident (*ʿaraḍ*), i.e. as a property of the omnipresent divine spirit (*rūḥ*) which brought the world into existence. FM.I: 55. Ibn ʿArabī thought it necessary for the universe as a whole to be alive since God made the world because 'He loved to be known' (FM.II: 399). 'Being alive is one of the conditions of being a knower (*ʿālim*). It is thus necessary for all things to be alive', Ibn ʿArabī said (FM.I: 636).

58 Every human has one soul only. The faculties of the human soul were sometimes referred to as the vegetable soul, desiring soul (*al-nafs al-shahwaniyya*), wrathful soul (*al-nafs al-ghadabiyya*) and the like in Ibn ʿArabī's works. On his side, Ibn ʿArabī's taught that the vegetable soul was responsible for the nourishment of the body. See FM.III: 237 and Rašić, *Bedeviled*, pp. 81–103.

59 Ibn ʿArabī, *K. ʿAnqāʾ mughrib*, p. 108; Ibn ʿArabī, *K. al-Tadbīrāt al-ilāhiyya*, p. 322.

60 See FM.I: 120, 247, 288; FM.II: 613 and Landau, *The Philosophy of Ibn Arabi*, p. 38.

61 Wolfe, *What Is Posthumanism?*, p. 40.

62 Wittgenstein, *The Wittgenstein Reader*, p. 213.

63 Dennett, *Kinds of Minds*, p. 18.

Ibn ʿArabī, for his part, drew attention to verses from the Qur'an describing the sentient nature of stones and mountains (e.g. Q. 17:44, 44:29). The possibility of their being capable of speech and reason thus cannot be (easily) dismissed in Sufi circles. On his side, Ibn ʿArabī taught that all things in existence were capable of speech. Finding a stone that *could not* speak would be a true miracle as a matter of fact. It is just that God made humans and jinn incapable of hearing the voices of minerals. 'No human or jinn can witness this unseen reality except when the laws of nature are broken [by sorcery] or unless God grants them special honour, trait or ability to access the knowledge of the Unseen,' Ibn ʿArabī maintained.[64] Lengthy spiritual retreats (*khalwāt*) and remembrance of God (*dhikr*) were the methods Ibn ʿArabī recommended to those seeking access to knowledge of the Unseen by pleasing Him. Spiritual seekers were advised to sit at the feet of an accomplished Sufi shaykh if nothing came of their retreats and sorceries. This was a foolproof method to hear the voices of minerals, Ibn ʿArabī claimed, citing the example of God's messenger Muhammad and his followers. For as long as they remained in the vicinity of the prophet, his followers could hear pebbles and mountains professing their love for God and Muhammad.[65] Sufi shaykh ʾAbū Madyan (d. 1198) was loved and admired by minerals as well.[66] To summarize, although Ibn ʿArabī deemed that minerals lacked unique character traits and personalities, he still thought them capable of:

- Fluent, grammatically correct speech
- Emotions such as love, fear, sadness and compassion
- Shedding tears, eating and breathing
- Receiving God's messengers and prophets
- Paying *zakat*, which is annual tax God imposed on Muslims
- Committing sin and engaging in religious worship.[67]

Ibn ʿArabī's views on the topic are the opposite of those of Sohn-Rethel and Slavoj Žižek, who were ready to acknowledge and discuss *only* the quantitative dimension of (gold) coins. The metal a coin is made of, Žižek

[64] FM.II: 682. See also FM.I: 521, 529; Ibn ʿArabī, *K. ʿAnqāʾ mughrib*, p. 141 and Elmore, 'The Fabulous Gryphon', p. 316.

[65] See FM.I: 120, 139–140, 288; Ibn ʿArabī, *K. al-yaqīn*, p. 49; Ibn ʿArabī, *ʿUqlat al-mustawfiz*, p. 122. Elsewhere, Ibn ʿArabī explained that voices of minerals do not resemble human speech in the least (because no stone has vocal cords, mouth and tongue). Angels, humans and jinn are the only species in existence with organs of speech. Minerals rather speak with the tongue of their essence (*lisān dhāt*). If one were to hear their speech, Ibn ʿArabī said, they would find it akin to a powerful, overwhelming presence. See Ibn ʿArabī, *Sharḥ tarjumān ashwāq*, p. 47.

[66] Ibn ʿArabī, *Kitab al-maʿarif*, pp. 255–256.

[67] Further information can be found at FM.I: 247, 529, 559, 583 and FM.II: 257.

said, is but a carrier of its social function, which is to serve as an embodiment of wealth, 'as a means of exchange and not as an object of use'.[68] Ibn ʿArabī was chiefly interested in qualitative dimensions as he worked on the elixir that could remove illnesses and defects preventing common stones and metals from turning into gold.

With the notable exception of the Qur'an, scriptures and studies in Islam did little to make the voices of minerals heard. It is the hallmark of humanism to focus on voices from the margins – the voices of the oppressed – 'but without in the least destabilizing or throwing into radical question the schema of the human who undertakes pluralization'.[69] Cary Wolfe identified this as one of the pitfalls of posthumanist studies, which revolve around humans speaking for nonhumans. Ibn ʿArabī *obviously* did not identify as a posthumanist, given that he passed away centuries before the movement rose to prominence. Yet some of his writings align with contemporary definitions of posthumanism, exposing him to similar criticism as a result. The confidence with which he discussed the thoughts, feelings and needs of minerals was rooted in the widely shared beliefs about the origins of alchemy in Muslim cultures and societies. This is the topic of the next section (Section 4).

4 Seek Knowledge, Even as Far as China!

The title of this section is based on the saying attributed to the prophet Muhammad: *aṭlubū al-ʿilm wa law fī al-Ṣīn*. Imperial edicts prohibiting alchemists from making counterfeit gold, which were issued by Emperor Jing of Han in 144 BC are among the earliest – if not the earliest – mentions of synthetic transmutations in history.[70] Knowledge of alchemy has been exchanged between China and India,[71] with the latter being regarded as the cradle of magic by Ibn ʿArabī.

[68] Žižek, *The Sublime Object of Ideology*, p. 13, 28. Cf. Sohn-Rethel, *Intellectual and Manual Labor*, p. 59.

[69] Wolfe, *What Is Posthumanism?*, p. 99.

[70] Ying Shao explained:

> Emperor Wen, in his fifth year (175 BC), allowed people to coin [cash], a law that had not yet been abrogated. At previous times there had been made much [alchemistic] counterfeit gold. [But] counterfeit gold cannot really be made, and vainly [causes] loss and expense, so that it turns to boasting about one's brilliancy. When [these alchemists] become poor, they rise up and turn to brigandry or robbery. Hence [Emperor] established this law.

Quoted according to Pan Ku, *The History of the Former Han Dynasty*, vol. 1, p. 323. Cf. Dubs, 'The Beginnings of Alchemy', p. 63 and Holmyard, *Alchemy*, p. 31.

[71] For instance, see Linden, *The Alchemy Reader*, p. 7.

There are records of Buddhist monks attempting to turn lesser metals into gold by infusing them with admixtures of herbs and mercury between the second and the fifth century.[72] Whether their work was a source of inspiration for the early Arab alchemists remains to be determined, however. 'The early history of Arabic alchemy', Charles Burnett observed, 'and the means by which it was transmitted to the West are topics as elusive as the Philosopher's Stone itself, and as passionately pursued'.[73] This is a topic for another book and decidedly another author. Our present concern is to identify the principal authorities that alchemists liked to invoke, as a step toward establishing a framework for the posthumanist approach to Akbarian studies.

The texts and creeds we will examine were dismissed as 'irrelevant' and 'fiction' by Julius Ruska and others.[74] Not even Ruska could deny, however, that Akbarian Sufism and Islam centre around the notions of divine, revealed knowledge (*kashf*) and the authorities built on unbroken chains of transmission (*isnād*) and authorization (*ijāzah*). This means that the major sources of religion in Islam are the holy Qur'an, which was revealed to the prophet Muhammad, and the hadith collections. Hadiths are the sayings attributed to God or Muhammad, which were (in)validated based on a chain of transmitters. For as long as the saying did not contradict the Qur'an, its content was valid but of secondary importance to compilers. Their primary concern was to identify every individual involved in transmitting it – for example, that a certain hadith reached us via venerable ʿAbū Nuʿaym, who heard it from another honorable man, Zakariyā', who heard it from the prophet Muhammad himself. Muslim alchemists adopted the same line of reasoning when emphasizing their manuals originate from Hermes, who entrusted them to Ostanes, who entrusted them to Democritus, who entrusted them to Maryam, and so on – until they eventually reached Jābir b. Ḥayyān, who is traditionally regarded as the father of alchemy in Muslim cultures and societies.[75] British alchemists,

[72] The monks in question referred to their craft as 'the science of mercury' (*raseśvaradarśana*). Sheppard, 'Alchemy: Origin or Origins?', p. 73. See also Rajan, 'Religion and the Development of an Alchemical Philosophy of Transmutation in Ancient India', pp. 101–102.

[73] Burnett, 'The Astrologer's Assay of the Alchemist', p. 103.

[74] See Ruska, *Tabula Smaragdina*, p. 52.

[75] The identity of Jābir b. Ḥayyān, the extent of the corpus attributed to him, and even the question of his historical existence are the subjects of passionate debates. The debates began before the tenth century AD and remain to be settled. Listing every argument and counterargument which were made over the course of centuries is beyond the scope of my Element – but I would like to direct the reader to the writings of Paul Kraus, who convincingly argued that the so-called Jabirian corpus was penned a full century after

such as William Backhouse and Elias Ashmole, valued spiritual lineage and bonds between master and disciple as well.[76] But whereas these elements have been disregarded when analysing the alchemical traditions of the West at times, Islam proved more resilient to attempts at evisceration and secularization. *Kashf*, *isnād* and *ijāzah* were essential to medieval jurisprudents and alchemists alike.

Now, Ibn ʿArabī's contemporaries differentiated between the so-called Arabic sciences, such as jurisprudence, rhetoric and grammar, and the foreign sciences (*ʿulūm al-ʿajam*) which were popularized through the Graeco-Arabic translation movement. Nearly *all* scholarly works that were available in the Byzantine Empire were translated into Arabic by the mid eight century.[77] Alchemical treatises were among them, although there were already several competing narratives on the transmission of the royal art by the tenth century. The most popular reports revolved around the Umayyad prince Khālid b. Yazīd (d. 709), who sought the knowledge of alchemy to enrich his friends and brothers. And so he summoned the wise monk Morienus from Alexandria and studied with him for a time. Then he sent for competent translators from Egypt and had them translate books on alchemy from Greek into Arabic, with Ibn al-Nadīm (d. 995) claiming 'this was the first translation in Islam from one language into another'.[78] There are scholars aplenty questioning the story of Khālid, with Ibn al-Nadīm himself providing several competing narratives explaining how Muslims turned alchemists. I could cite them all, pointing out inconsistencies and surmising which one might be closest to the truth, but I will not. For those interested, they are readily available in Dodge's translation of *Fihrist*. I would like to highlight two details from Ibn al-Nadīm's story of Khālid instead: first, that the Graeco-Arabic translation movement introduced alchemy to Muslim cultures and societies according to the story; and second, that Egypt played a central role in supplying books, teachers

Jābir's presumed date of death (Kraus, *Alchemie, Ketzerei, Apokryphen in frühen Islam*). Seyyed Hossain Nasr is among the most prominent supporters of the theory there was a man named Jābir, who *was* the founder of Islamic alchemy and a disciple of the sixth Shia imam Jaʿfar al-Ṣādiq. For instance, see Nasr (ed.), *Ismaili Thought in the Classical Age*, pp. 6, 35–37. Cf. Haq, *Names, Natures and Things*, p. 3, 25.

[76] Ashmole studied with William Backhouse (d. 1662), who was his 'alchemical father'. Close ties between 'alchemical fathers' and their 'sons' in Europe, Bruce Janacek explained, are comparable to initiation into the priesthood. This initiation is the root of the alchemical power to cleanse and purify the world of nature. Janacek, *Alchemical Belief*, pp. 1–2.

[77] Further information on the Graeco-Arabic translation movement and the so-called Arabic and foreign sciences can be found at Gutas, *Greek Thought, Arabic Culture*, pp. 1, 28–61.

[78] Ibn al-Nadīm, *The Fihrist*, vol. 2, p. 581.

and translators. The first premise has been verified time and again.[79] The second remains a subject of disputes to date.

John Read argued that Egypt was the motherland of chemistry for a reason. Ancient Egyptians were accomplished in metallurgy, glassware and gold-smithing, and they were working with alloys as early as the third millennium BC.[80] Plutarch reported they named their land 'Chemia' in reference to its black soil, which resembles the colour of the pupil,[81] and there are scholars surmising that the Arabic word *al-kīmīyā'* was derived from the historical, former name of Egypt.[82] *Corpus Hermeticum* described Egypt as an image of heaven and the fountain of all knowledge (including alchemy).[83] It is worth noting, however, that no books on alchemy in Ancient Egyptian have been discovered to date. The earliest surviving treatises were written in the early Roman imperial period in Greek.[84] Arab alchemists did not readily acknowledge their indebtedness to Byzantium, Greece and Rome, however: it was politically inconvenient to do so. They were also captivated by the allure of pharaonic Egypt, much like Greek philosophers before them. It is questionable whether alchemical lore or Plato's reports on Atlantis would have been taken seriously had they been attributed to Solon, the Athenian lawmaker, rather than the priests of Egypt he consulted (or claimed to have consulted). Plato's dialogue *Timaeus* contains the following exchange between Solon and Sonchis, the priest of Saïs:

> Ah, Solon, Solon, you Greeks are ever children. There isn't an old man among you.' On hearing this, Solon said, 'What? What do you mean?' 'You are young,' the old priest replied, 'young in soul, every

[79] The direct link between the Graeco-Arabic translation movement and the growing interest in alchemy in Muslim cultures and societies has been long established in scholarly literature. Kevin van Bladel remains hopeful, however, that further research might prove his suspicion at least *some* Arabic works on alchemy were based on translations from Middle Persian, rather than Greek. Van Bladel, *The Arabic Hermes*, p. 30. Persians were infamous in Muslim cultures and societies for dabbling in demonology and magic and there are records suggesting that Babylonians were attempting to make silver from the admixture of bronze and coper as early as the thirteenth century BC. See Debus, *The Chemical Promise*, p. 24 and Braun, 'Who Began this Art?', p. 386.

[80] Linden, *The Alchemy Reader*, p. 5.

[81] Plutarch, *Moralia V*, p. 83.

[82] John Read and Titus Burckhard proposed that alchemy may have been named after Egypt. The latter, however, also allowed the possibility that the word alchemy comes from the Syriac *kīmīyā*, which in its turn goes back to the Greek χυμεία or χημεία, 'the art of casting or alloying metals'. The term 'alchemy' was incorporated into the Latin language around 1151 AD. See Braun, 'Who Began This Art', p. 375; Burckhardt, *Alchemy*, p. 16, Burnett, 'The Astrologer's Assay of the Alchemist', p. 104. and Linden, *The Alchemy Reader*, p. 5.

[83] Scott (ed.), *Hermetica*, vol. 1, p. 341.

[84] Beretta, *Alchemy of Glass*, 8–22, 40–47; Martelli, 'Translating Ancient Alchemy', p. 3; Martelli-Rumor, *Near Eastern Origins of Graeco-Egyptian Alchemy*, p. 37.

one of you. Your souls are devoid of beliefs about antiquity handed down by ancient tradition. Your souls lack any learning made hoary by time.'[85]

The quoted paragraph echoes humanity's perennial, naïve longings for the wisdom of bygone eras and faraway lands. Effective, authentic spiritual practices and philosophies must be rooted in age-old tradition: they cannot be both new *and* true. Celsus used this argument against Christianity in AD 170.[86] The Church Fathers mocked Islam for being a late and derivative religion in turn.[87] Muslim proponents of the Graeco-Arabic translation movement deliberately invoked the term *ʿulūm al-qudamāʾ*, the sciences of the ancients, as they sought to convince the hostile ulema of their merit.[88] Alchemists in particular linked their work and expertise to Hermes.

Hermes appears in Ibn al-Nadīm's list of the fifty-two alchemists who failed to concoct the elixir that could turn lesser metals into gold.[89] Still, he had admirers aplenty among Arabs, who referred to him as Hermes Thrice Endowed with Wisdom (*Hermes al-Muthalath bil-Ḥikma*). Ancient Egyptians bestowed similar titles on the ibis-headed Thot, whose counterpart was the Greek god Hermes.[90] In Arabic texts, Hermes's sobriquet could serve to indicate that he was both king, priest and philosopher *or* that there were three scholars worthy of consideration whose personal name was 'Hermes'. The oldest of the three lived before the Flood, the second was Babylonian and the third was Egyptian. Medieval chronicles

---

[85] Plato, *Timaeus*, p. 33. Although there are no records of him attempting to turn common stones and metals into gold, numerous alchemical treatises have been associated with Plato in Muslim cultures and societies. Gold-smelting was a synonym for misguided efforts in Plato's works, however. See Linden, *The Alchemy Reader*, p. 29 and Lindsay, *The Origins of Alchemy in Graeco-Roman Egypt*, pp. 27–29.

[86] Hanegraaf, *Western Esotericism*, p. 48. Cf. Origen, *Contra Celsum*, p. 209, 289.

[87] For instance, see St John of Damascus, *Writings*, pp. 153–160.

[88] This was most probably a wise decision. The beginning of an end of mainstream alchemical and hermetical pursuits in Europe, Wouter Hanegraaf noted, was in 1614, when Isaac Casaubon demonstrated that the text of *Corpus Hermeticum* was written no earlier than the second century AD. The intellectual credibility of alchemists never recovered from the blow. Hanegraaf, *Western Esotericism*, p. 120.

[89] Ibn al-Nadīm, *The Fihrist*, vol. 2, p. 850. See also Stapleton, 'The Sayings Attributed to Hermes', p. 69.

[90] The earliest hieroglyphic inscriptions celebrating the thrice-great god Thot (*Ḏḥwty ꜣ ꜣ ꜣ wr nb Ḫmnw*) were discovered at the temple of Edfu and dated around 204–181 BC. He was also known as the twice-great lord of Hermopolis during the twenty-sixth dynasty (664–525 BC), and in the third century BC the Flinders-Petrie papyrus described him as the five-times greatest Thot. Bull, *The Tradition of Hermes Trismegustus*, pp. 33–35. See also Chassinat, *Le temple d'Edfou*, vol. 6, p. 230; Gauthier-Sottas, *Un décret trilingue en l'honneur de Ptolémée IV*, p. 72 and Ritner, 'Hermes Pentamegistos', pp. 73–75.

focused on the first Hermes for the most part and not a few scholars thought him the same person as Idris the Prophet. He was rumoured to be the first human to wear sewn clothes, write with a pen and conduct astronomical observations (among other things). Alchemists believed God ordered Idris/Hermes to see to it that his knowledge survived the cataclysmic flood that wiped out the giants from Earth. A man of his wisdom knew that stone was more durable than paper and resistant to water. Thus, he had his teachings engraved to the walls of pyramids. Abū Maʿshār (d. 886) said:

> His home was in the Upper Egypt; he chose that [place] and built the pyramids and cities of clay there. He feared that knowledge would pass away in the Flood, so he built the monumental temples (*al-barābī*); it is a mountain known as *birbā* in Akhmim, which he chiseled out, portraying in it in carvings all the arts and their uses, and pictures of all the instruments of the artisans, indicating the features of the sciences by illustrations, out of desire thereby to preserve the sciences forever for those after him, fearing that all trace of it would perish from the world. It is reported by the account transmitted from the early Muslims (*as-salaf*) that Idrīs was the first to study books, to investigate the sciences. God sent thirty scrolls (*ṣaḥīfa*) down to him.[91]

The temple complex of Akhmim was among the largest in Egypt. Nothing remains of it, however, since Sultan al-Nāṣir Muḥammad (d. 1314) had it demolished because he needed stones for a mosque. Ibn Jubayr described the temple as a marvel to behold two centuries before the building frenzy took over the sultan.[92] Dhū al-Nūn Miṣrī (d. 862), Zosimos of Panopolis and Buṭrus al-Ḥakīm are among the sages who frequented the complex. To master alchemy, Ibn Umayl (d. 960) suggested, one must go to Akhmim and learn from Hermes directly, by studying his engravings that could be found there. Ibn Umayl liked copying hieroglyphs himself.[93] The formal writing system of Ancient

[91] Quoted according to von Bladel, *The Arabic Hermes*, p. 126. Von Bladel amassed excerpts from the earliest extant Islamic works on Hermes by Abū Maʿshār Balkhī (d. 886), Ibn Juljūl (d. 994), Ibn al-Qifṭī (d. 1248), Ibn Abī Uṣāybiʿa (d. 1270) and others. Excerpts are given in both English and Arabic, describing the three Hermeses, Hermes as the builder of pyramids and the master of all sciences, Hermes as the counterpart of Idris the Prophet, etc. See Bladel, *The Arabic Hermes*, pp. 121–241. Cf. Plessner, 'Hermes Trismegistus and Arab Sciences', p. 51 and Reeves, *Enoch from Antiquity to the Middle Ages*, vol. 1, p. 65, 67–68.

[92] Ibn Jubayr, *The Travels of Ibn Jubayr*, p. 55. See also Derchain-Urtel, 'Thot at Akhmim', pp. 173–180.

[93] Ibn Umayl, *Durra an- naqlya*, pp. 40–41, 93; Richter, 'The Master Spoke', p. 167. Akhmim was a major center of the dyeing industry since the ancient times, which was traditionally linked with alchemy. See MacCoull, 'Coptic Alchemy', p. 101 and Martelli, *The Four Books*, pp. 68–69.

Egypt combined ideographic, logographic, syllabic and alphabetic elements. In his works, Abū Maʿshār mistook hieroglyphs for drawings (*ṣuwar*) made by Hermes. His views were shared by Ibn Waḥshiyya (d. 930), who believed that the following hieroglyphs contained the secrets of minerals (Figure 2). Ibn Waḥshiyya maintained that an accomplished spiritual seeker could grasp the meaning of these and other hieroglyphs at a glance. He supplied translations for the uninitiated in his book *K. Shawq al-mustahām*, but only of those hieroglyphs he knew 'to be exact

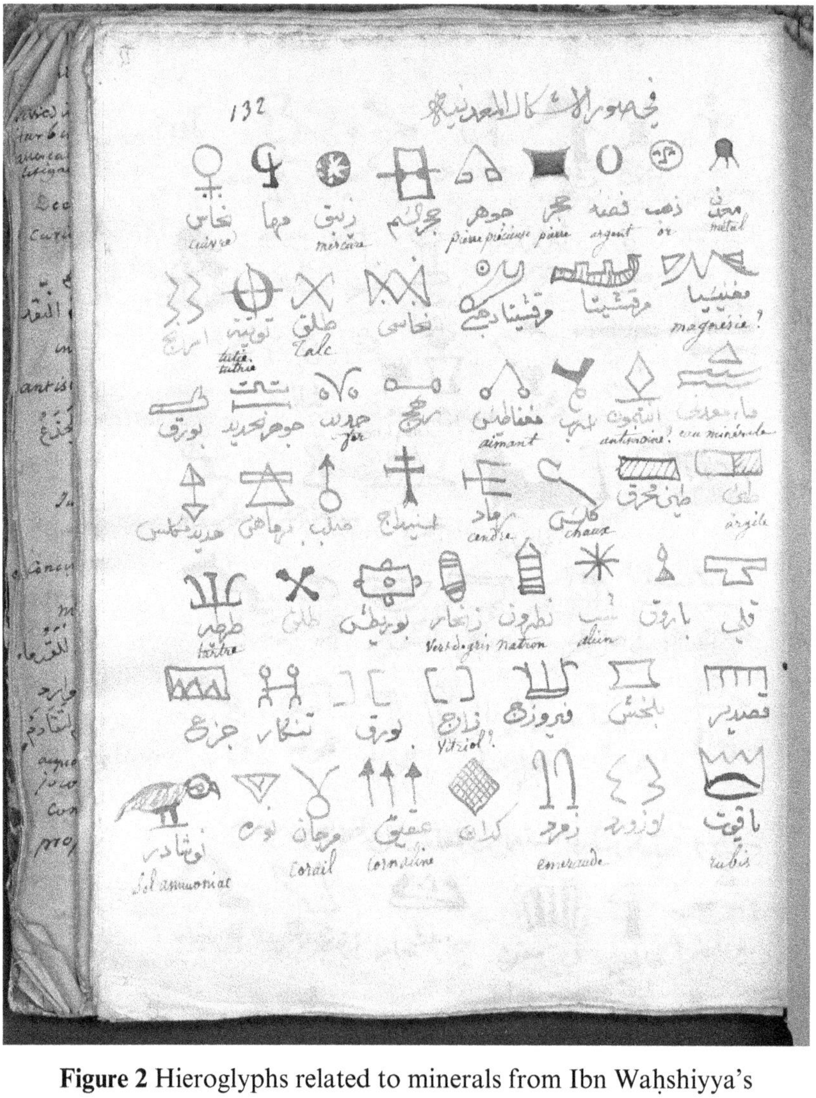

Figure 2 Hieroglyphs related to minerals from Ibn Waḥshiyya's *K. Shawq al-mustahām* (BSB Cod.arab. 789, ff. 132. Munich: Bayerische StaatsBibliothek, 1791).

and right. Perhaps every one of these figures may have had more than one signification, according to the different classes of priests, who wishing to hide their secrets one from the other, game their signs different meanings.'[94] Ancient Egyptians were fond of synonyms of metaphors to be sure, but they are not to be blamed for *every* comical misreading of hieroglyphic inscriptions – like when Abū al-Qāsim al-ʿIrāqī mistook a stela celebrating king Amenemhat II of Egypt as Horus reborn for instructions from Hermes concerning the use of distillation furnace in the First Operation of blackening.[95] Medieval readers would have blamed such misinterpretations on the spiritual proves of alchemists (or the lack of thereof), for it was once widely accepted that the cryptic form of hieroglyphs was meant to protect Hermes's teachings from the unworthy. *Epistles of the Brethren of Purity* in particular explained that the knowledge of alchemy would corrupt the souls of the common folk by infusing them with greed and caprice. Hence the need for secrecy and obfuscation.[96]

Ibn ʿArabī had a somewhat different opinion on drawings and diagrams of accomplished spiritual seekers. Spiritual messages can be difficult to put in words at times, he said. Some sages thus rely on visual arts to convey their teachings directly to the heart of a student via imagination:

> The disciple will represent in himself the spiritual meaning (*maʿnā*) in materialized form, thus facilitating its explicit expression by having it integrated into his imagination. The one who considers [the spiritual meaning in materialized form] will then aspire to complete his consideration and get to know the totality of its spiritual meanings. This is due to the fact that sensation (*al-ḥiss*), once it's poured into the mold of form and figure (*qālab al-ṣūra wa al-shakl*), is taken with the spiritual reality. The disciple finds pleasure in it, it provides him with delight – and this leads him to realize what manifests to him the figure and what materializes to him by this form.[97]

Was Ibn ʿArabī familiar with the works of Ibn Waḥshiyya, whose views on the visual arts he shared? Perhaps. Both his cryptographs and the symbols he used in his talismans bear resemblance to scrawls and doodles

[94] See Ibn Waḥshiyya, *Ancient Alphabets*, p. 16, 36, 40.

[95] Also known as nigredo, blackening is the first step in the process of creating the philosopher's stone in laboratory settings. It refers to putrefaction and/or decomposition of alchemical components, which are then exposed to cleansing agents and fire to form a uniform black matter. Abraham, *A Dictionary of Alchemical Imagery*, pp. 10, 20–21. Further information on al-ʿIrāqī's attempt at translating the stela of Amenemhat II of Egypt can be found at the British Museum, 'A Medieval Alchemical Book Reveals New Secrets', blog, 5 February 2016, www.britishmuseum.org/blog/medieval-alchemical-book-reveals-new-secrets.

[96] Brethren of Purity, *On Magic*, p. 143.

[97] Ibn ʿArabī, *Inshāʾ al-dawāʾir*, p. 6.

from *K. Shawq al-mustahām*.[98] Ibn ʿArabī did not concern himself with Ibn Waḥshiyya's attempts to translate hieroglyphs, however. Although he passed through Egypt on his way to Mecca, there is no evidence to suggest he took a detour to Akhmim to search for surviving messages from Hermes. Stephen Hirtenstein argued that he went straight from Cairo to Palestine in June 1202.[99] There are no surviving records of Ibn ʿArabī exploring the Giza pyramid complex either, which was linked to Hermes in classical literature,[100] and he seemingly passed on the opportunity to consult with local alchemists in Cairo. Had he wished to, Ibn ʿArabī had every chance to learn from accomplished scholars in his homeland, Andalusia.

Our understanding of the early history of alchemy in Spain owes much to the meticulous research of Juan Alegre. Hermes Trismegistos, the thrice-great Hermes, came to Spain twice according to him. That is to say, Alegre identified two cultural movements that popularized alchemical books and practices in Spain. The first can be dated to late antiquity and the beginning of the Christian Middle Ages, when Priscillian, the bishop of Avilla, worked his magic with precious stones and demons. Other references to alchemy in late Roman Hispania include the *Etymologies* of Isidore of Seville (d. 636), who wrote after the Visigoth takeover. The second arrival of Hermes, Alegre said, came to pass after the Muslim conquest of the Iberian Peninsula in the early eighth century. Extensive 'orientalization' of the peninsula took place during the reign of al-Ḥakam I (796–822) and ʿAbd al-Raḥmān II (822–852), who tried as hard as they might to emulate the cultural splendour of Baghdad. Setting up a clique of court astrologers was a part of their efforts. Among them was ʿAbbās b. Firnās (d. 887), a physician, engineer and a role model for the generations of alchemists to come. Firnās was also well versed in *nīranjāt*, which is a type of sorcery rooted in Pseudo-Aristotelian *Hermetica*.[101] Ibn ʿArabī was no stranger to dark arts such as *nīranjāt* and *ʿuzābīyyah*. Yet he proudly stated he did not cite a single scholar in his works.[102] Ibn

[98] See Ibn ʿArabī, *K. al-Tajalliyāt* (MS Veliyuddin #1759), ff. 21, 80 and Rašić, *The Written World of God*, pp. 13–14, 33, 54–55.

[99] Hirtenstein, *The Unlimited Mercifier*, p. 147.

[100] For instance, Ibn al-Nadīm identified Hermes as the builder of the Giza pyramid complex. The three pyramids were purportedly meant to serve as a grave for Hermes, his wife and son. Ibn al-Nadīm, *The Fihrist*, vol. 2, p. 845. Shaddād b. ʿĀd, the evil lord of Iram, and Sorid, the king of Egypt, have been also identified as the builders of the pyramids in Arabic literature. See Fodor, 'The Origins of Arabic Legends', p. 335 and Graefe (trans.), *Das Pyramidenkapitel in Al-Makrīzī's "Ḫiṭaṭ"*, p. 93.

[101] Alegre, *The Spanish Hermes*, p. 6, 21–24. Further information on Priscillian can be found in Burrus, *The Making of a Heretic*.

[102] FM.II: 432.

ʿArabī maintained that his knowledge of alchemy did not come from books but revelations. 'I know [God's] greatest name and alchemy by means of revelation (*munāzala* or *tanazzul*), and not through acquisition,' he said.[103]

Now, there are paragraphs Ibn ʿArabī wrote that bear resemblance to the works of his predecessors. His views on the generation and corruption of minerals, for instance, appear to be based on the writings of Aristotle and Jābir. Samer Dajani claimed that Ibn ʿArabī appropriated pages upon pages from *Bidāya al-mujtahid* by Ibn Rushd (d. 1198).[104] There is no shortage of self-proclaimed 'plagiarism hunters' today, who would happily argue this warrants complete rejection of Ibn ʿArabī's masterpiece *al-Futūḥāt*, where the 'transgression' occurred, and all his other books besides. Ibn ʿArabī would have likely countered that nobody holds the monopoly on truth, had he had a chance to plead his case. Truth is primordial and universal by nature, and not necessarily original. Divine revelations in particular transcend space and time and similarities between revealed knowledge and human attempts at philosophy are not a proof of derivation. Instead, they ought to be taken as a confirmation that philosophers sometimes got things right. When Muhammad was sent to correct scriptures from the times past, a part of his mission included retelling familiar stories from the Bible and the Torah as they really happened.[105] It is well known that Muhammad was instructed by the archangel Gabriel on God's order. But who was the teacher of Ibn ʿArabī, who revealed the knowledge of alchemy to him?

Jaime Flequer argued that Ibn ʿArabī first learned alchemy from Jesus,[106] who is recognized as one of God's prophets in Islam, with the ability to bring clay figurines to life (Q 3:49, 5:110). Flequer's theory does not seem implausible in the light of the fact that Ibn ʿArabī argued that the knowledge of bestowing life and form – *kun fa-yakūn* – is indispensable for alchemists. Ibn ʿArabī claimed to have conversed with Jesus over the course of his journey through the seven heavens. Here, I would advise the reader to return to Figure 1, to better visualize Ibn ʿArabī's ascent through the heavenly spheres. At every heaven, a Muslim prophet awaited to share certain knowledge and insights with him. Ibn ʿArabī identified the second heaven, which is the Sphere of Mercury, as the

[103] Quoted according to Hirtenstein (ed.), *Muhyiddin Ibn Arabi*, p. 309.

[104] Dajani, *Sufis and Sharīʿa*, p. 107.

[105] Now, *why* would God allow humans to corrupt His scriptures? Ibn ʿArabī professed himself in the dark on the matter. FM.III: 351.

[106] Flequer 'The Science of Letters', p. 12

domain of Jesus and Yahya. These two prophets know all about the act of genesis, magic, measure and meter. Jesus and Yahya can also teach alchemists how miracles are performed and how the same idea can take many different forms. Without this knowledge, no alchemist would go far.[107] The quest for red sulphur, however, dictates that other heavens are to be visited as well. Although Jesus was one of Ibn ʿArabī's teachers, he was neither the first nor the primary source of information guiding his works on alchemy.

Before a spiritual seeker can reach Jesus at the Sphere of Mercury, they must traverse the Sphere of the Moon. This is the realm of Adam and the lowest of the seven heavens. Under the guidance of Adam, alchemists begin learning about metallurgy and minerology. Adam will also teach them about duties of God's viceregent on Earth, which include acting as an agent of divine knowledge, overseeing the visible world and fostering the transformation and growth of minerals. This prophet knows the secret of happiness, and the exact nature of the relationship between the elixir of felicity, which every alchemist seeks to concoct, and the self-disclosures of God. Having received instructions from Adam, Jesus and Yahya, an aspiring alchemist must proceed to the Sphere of Venus to learn about life-force, and the generation and corruption of minerals. Joseph, who is the prophet in charge of this sphere, will also instruct them about working with masses and meters, and celestial spheres and orbits. As Section 5 will demonstrate, this knowledge is essential for turning lesser metals into gold. Further above is the Sphere of the Sun, where alchemists must learn about the visible world and the Unseen from Idris/Hermes. Those who manage to reach the Sphere of the Sun will also be informed about the perfect nature of minerals, and they will receive in-depth knowledge about the seven climes, the revolution of celestial spheres and their impact on Earth. Then comes the Sphere of Mars, where alchemists must learn about blood sacrifice, and how faith differs from fact from Aaron and David. At the Sphere of Jupiter, Moses will teach them the essences (*aʿyān*) of minerals, plants and animals. Once, long ago, sorcerers of the pharaoh used this knowledge to make their sticks appear as if they were snakes. This event is famously described in the Qur'an (Q. 115–118), with Ibn ʿArabī claiming that alchemists rely on the same techniques to turn marble pillars into gold. We will return to Ibn ʿArabī's alchemical syllabus in Sections 5 and 6. Now, our gaze turns to the Sphere of Saturn, 'desolate and wild', where Abraham awaits to impart instructions on cleansing the corporeal

107 See FM.I: 155 and FM.II: 274.

form and the soul of minerals.[108] This is where Muhammad met Gabriel, as he journeyed through the seven heavens. Ibn ʿArabī had to ascend even higher to meet Muhammad himself, in the vicinity of God's throne.[109]

The knowledge of alchemy was chiefly linked to Muhammad in Ibn ʿArabī's works. He described it as the First Mystery (*awwal sirr*), which God revealed to Muhammad in the first eon (*al-dahr al-awwal*), 'from which every subsequent aeon came into existence'.[110] Needless to say, the revelation did not occur in the seventh century AD, when Muhammad rallied his followers in Mecca and Medina. Muhammad famously claimed he was chosen by God to serve as His prophet before Adam was created, before the world was created (*Jāmiʿ al-Tirmidī* #3609). The First Mystery was revealed to him before the dawn of time. Alchemy was thought to be a science older than China, older than Egypt in Akbarian circles. Hence Ibn ʿArabī's lack of interest in wandering the ruins of Akhmim. His students were advised to seclude themselves from the world and engage in remembrance of God to prepare themselves for ascension through the heavenly spheres, where the first and the greatest human expert on the First Mystery awaits.

Shorter chains of transmission were preferred to long ones in Islam and the trustworthiness of transmitters was of no small importance either. Egyptian alchemist ʿIzz al-Dīn al-Jildakī (d. 1342) prided himself that his knowledge reached him from Adam, who transmitted it to Seth, who transmitted it to Hermes, who transmitted it to Noah, whose descendants transmitted it to Abraham, whose descendants entrusted it to Moses, who was one of the teachers of Jesus, who entrusted his knowledge to Muhammad, who was the teacher of Alī b. Abī Ṭālib, whose teachings were transmitted through the series of intermediaries to Jaʿfar al-Ṣādiq and Jābir.[111] Distinguished hadith compilers, such as Muslim b. al-Ḥajjāj (d. 875) and imam al-Bukhārī (d. 870), would have laughed at the recounted chain of transmission, which is both long and filled with gaps revolving around anonymous descendants of Noah, Abraham and Moses.

108 FM.I: 155–156; FM.II: 270–284. *Epistles of the Brethren of Purity* purported that Hermes himself also learned alchemy at the Sphere of Saturn: 'And so, it is related about Hermes the thrice-endowed with wisdom – and who is the prophet Idris, may peace be upon him – that he ascended to the sphere of Saturn and revolved with it for thirty years until he witnessed all the states of the celestial sphere. Then he descended back to earth and instructed people about star-lore.' Quoted according to Reeves, *Enoch from Antiquity to the Middle Ages*, vol. 1, p. 69.

109 For instance, see FM.I: 1–2.

110 FM.I: 152.

111 Zirnis, 'The Kitāb Ustuquss al-Uss of Jabir b. Ḥayyān', p. 57.

Over the course of centuries, hadiths have been discarded for less. What was not good enough for hadith compilers was not good enough for Ibn ʿArabī either. If anything, he held his sources to even higher standards.

Sufi scholars evaluated books and teachers differently than the sorcerers and philosophers Ibn ʿArabī encountered. We previously established that Ibn ʿArabī did not differentiate between the miracles performed by Sufis and sorcerers for the most part – and we also cited his definition of philosophy as the love of wisdom in Section 2. At no point did Ibn ʿArabī argue a Sufi loves wisdom less than a philosopher by training. Yet he sometimes differentiated between philosophers, Sufis and sorcerers based on, first, their character traits and, second, the methods they employed to gain a working knowledge of alchemy. The word 'philosopher' (*faylasūf*) was thus used in Ibn ʿArabī's works to denote a person with little or no inclination toward spiritual practices, who relies on their thoughts (*afkār*) and intellect (*ʿaql*) to advance in knowledge. Intellect is the chief authority a philosopher acknowledges,[112] even as they profess their devotion to long-dead sages, their arcane books and inscriptions buried in sand in some faraway land. A typical philosopher is self-sufficient, determined and proud. I have little to learn from my contemporaries, whose knowledge is but a shadow of what was lost before, a philosopher might say – and not even the best of them have had access to revealed knowledge.[113] This is what makes them different from Sufis.

I aspire to learn about the First Mystery like Muhammad, a Sufi would say, which would make it possible for me to imbue bodies and spirits with the perfection of gold. If I am worthy, God will reveal it to me directly or allow me to ascend to the higher heavens, where this knowledge can be gained from His prophets. Those who have access to revealed knowledge have no need to rely on books. We have already seen how Ibn ʿArabī identified Sufism with obedience to God and proper moral conduct, which are the defining character traits of a Sufi. This is what grants them access to revealed knowledge and the seven heavens. Sufi shaykhs commit their knowledge to paper at times, which is then plundered by sorcerers.

---

112 Ibn ʿArabī, *K. al-Isfār*, p. 46. Ibn ʿArabī's views on individual philosophers such as Plato, Aristotle and the like were examined in Rosenthal, 'Ibn ʿArabī between 'Philosophy' and "Mysticism"', pp. 1–35.

113 Spiritual knowledge and insights can be roughly divided into three categories in Ibn ʿArabī's works: 1) knowledge of the intellect (*ʿilm al-ʿaql*); 2) knowledge of the states (*ʿilm al-aḥwāl*), which was identified with experiencing the bitterness and/or sweetness of certain spiritual mysteries directly, as if by the means of senses; and 3) revealed knowledge of divine mysteries (*ʿilm al-asrār*). FM.I: 31. Philosophers concern themselves with rational knowledge.

Again, Ibn ʿArabī did not differentiate between alchemical transmutations performed by Sufi shaykhs and sorcerers. He did not think it necessary to label the former 'saintly miracles', as opposed to 'magic'. That being said, the word 'sorcerer' was used in his works as a synonym for a plethora of blameworthy character traits (*ṣifāt madhmūma*): greed, arrogance, wrath and the will to dominate. Most such people cannot be counted among God's friends, and they have no access to revealed knowledge (there are some exceptions to the general rule, however, which is not the case with philosophers!).[114] Being barred from heaven, a sorcerer must seek knowledge of alchemy elsewhere – and they will plunder it indiscriminately from books old and new, other humans and demons. The world is imbued with power, a sorcerer might say. All I need to learn is how to harness it – and God be damned! He will be dealt with if He dares stand in my way, for the world must bend to my will.

A philosopher's quest for red sulphur is chiefly driven by intellectual curiosity; Sufis are driven by altruism and sorcerers by the will to power. Ibn ʿArabī's learning method adhered to the Sufi path. Although he admired Ibn Rushd and wrote poetry in his honour, at no point did he forget that no human can compare to God. Ibn ʿArabī claimed to have been among the chosen few who got a chance to learn from Him. Thus, he refused to cite 'the words of philosophers nor the words of anyone else in *al-Futūḥāt.* In this book and all our books, we only ever write what is given to us by unveiling and what is dictated by God.'[115] In other words, God was his primary source of information on alchemy, and the thoughts and desires of minerals.

God is also the One speaking on behalf of minerals in Ibn ʿArabī's works, occasionally allowing the precious stones and metals to speak for themselves – with Ibn ʿArabī recording His words faithfully, with the help of scribes. This allows us to abandon the anthropocentric point of view in Islamic context, for it is God, rather than humans, who is undertaking the pluralization and allowing for a more diverse point of view in Sufi works on alchemy and in the Qur'an. This is the pinnacle of posthumanist studies, as Wolfe saw it.[116] Humans will play the role of observers in every alchemical transmutation discussed in this Element. The path forward now demands we identify the roots of corruption in minerals, which necessitate for transmutations to occur.

---

[114] See FM.II: 134–135, as well as Rašić, 'Fatima, the Righteous Sorceress', pp. 364–381 and Rašić, 'Masters of Dark Arts', pp. 1–10.

[115] FM.II: 432.

[116] Wolfe, *What Is Posthumanism?*, p. 99.

5 The Roots of Corruption

Heinrich Cornelius Agrippa (d. 1535) worked as a mining engineer and oversaw Habsburg silver mines in Freiberg, Saxony. He was hardly a stereotypical Renaissance alchemist, however. Most of his contemporaries sought never to get their hands dirty. The grit of mining and the grime of metallurgy they gladly left to others – a stand Agrippa and Paracelsus both criticized, since their inquiries led them to believe a successful transmutation hinges on in-depth knowledge of mineralogy and metallurgy.[117] Ibn ᶜArabī was not of the same opinion.

A sorcerer need not rely on knowledge to bend the world to their will. Alchemical transmutations can be accomplished by the means of *himma* – which is the term Ibn ᶜArabī used for spiritual powers and abilities of both God and humans.[118] Not every sorcerer understands the forces they set in motion, with Ibn ᶜArabī recommending his readers to familiarize themselves with the stages of a controlled alchemical transmutation (*tadbīr*).[119] This knowledge is more noble than the act of bringing precious stones and metals into existence through *himma*, he said.[120] Neither ignorance nor stupidity will prevent a sorcerer from turning iron into gold, however, provided they have power in abundance. The power cultivation techniques Ibn ᶜArabī described fall outside the scope of my Element, which adopts a posthumanist approach centring around minerals, rather than humans.

This Element previously established that the transmutation of mineral bodies is a side effect of their spiritual practices, which can be enhanced by exposure to red sulphur and *himma*. Synthetic transmutations which rely on *himma* have one major disadvantage: the miracle will only last for as long as a sorcerer can focus on maintaining it. The gold they made will become iron again or vanish the moment their concentration weavers.[121] Permanent alchemical transmutations almost always necessitate the presence of red sulphur, which is the topic for another section (Section 7). Our present goal is to examine the spiritual practices of minerals and the roots of corruption they must annihilate to become gold.

---

117 Paracelsus, *The Hermetic and Alchemical Writings*, p. 28. Agrippa's views on the matter were studied in Grafton, *Magus*, p. 200.

118 Ibn ᶜArabī, K. *Shaqq al-jayb*, p. 324; FM.II: 420–421. Further information on Ibn ʿArabī's views on *himma* can be found in Lala, 'Turning Religious Experience into Reality', pp. 1–16 and Rašić, 'Masters of Dark Arts', pp. 3–4.

119 FM.II: 46. Hirtenstein determined that solution (*taḥlīl*), distillation (*taṣʿīd*) and sublimation (taqtīr) of minerals are the stages Ibn ᶜArabī had in mind. Hirtenstein (trans.), *The Alchemy of Human Happiness*, p. 27.

120 FM.II 460–461.

121 Ibn ᶜArabī, *Bezels of Wisdom*, p. 102.

Ibn ʿArabī underlined the tendency of comparing the human heart to minerals, both in the Qur'anic Arabic and in the everyday speech of Arabs. For instance, there are verses in the Qur'an describing how God made iron mouldable for David (Q. 34:10). As iron is softened by fire, God's admonishments and warnings can soften the human heart – this is how Ibn ʿArabī interpreted the tenth verse of the surah *Sabāʾ*. Fire will not soften stone, however, and hardships can likewise harden the heart like stone.[122] A virtuous heart has been compared to a bronze mirror, polished and shined, in Sufi literature – and the prophet Muhammad taught that sins cause the human heart to blacken and rust (*Ibn Majah* #4244). To reach God, a spiritual seeker must cleanse their heart, as well as their eyes, ears, tongue, hands, stomach, sexual organs and feet. There are many different paths to God, however, and many different methods a person could employ to ascend. The natural disposition of a human being determines the furthest point of their spiritual ascension, as well as the path to God that is the most suited for them to follow.[123] Spiritual and bodily configuration of minerals differ significantly to that of humans, popular metaphors notwithstanding. Thus, it would be wrong to assume their path to God can be divided into the same step-levels (*marātib*), states (*aḥwāl*) and spiritual stations (*maqāmāt*) a human must traverse. In rare cases, a mineral may traverse a spiritual station that is also available to humans – and one such example would be the station of *tawba*, which is the station of turning to God in repentance – the account it would give of that station would not alight with human experiences of *tawba*.[124] Nevertheless, submission to Islam is one thing minerals and humans can have in common.

Next to nothing is known about God's messengers and prophets who were sent to the kingdom of minerals before Muhammad, although their existence is affirmed in the Qur'an. 'For every community there is a messenger', the surah *al-Yūnus* reads (Q. 10:47), 'who lived in this community' (Q. 35:24). Minerals form a community as well, and the same goes for 'all living beings that roam on earth and soar in the sky' (Q. 6:38). Not all messengers who preached to the kingdom of minerals were human, with Ibn ʿArabī claiming that God appointed ants as His prophets to guide ant colonies. Omniscient, He knew that ants – like minerals and jinn – would be more inclined to obey a member of their own species, rather than Solomon.[125] The prophets of ants and jinn had nothing to say to humans,

[122] Ibn ʿArabī, *Bezels of Wisdom*, p. 205.
[123] Ibn ʿArabī, *K. al-khalwa*, pp. 33–34. See also Rašić, *The Nightfolk*, pp. 83–85.
[124] FM.II: 142–143.
[125] FM.I: 83.

and we know nothing of their teachings as a result. Muhammad was different, however. His mission was to bring divine knowledge and mercy to every community in existence, so minerals, plants and animals – and wicked jinn besides! – counted themselves among his followers.[126] Ibn ʿArabī did not approve of those who claimed that minerals have no knowledge of Islam.

Every living being other than humans and jinn is instinctively drawn towards the Divine, Ibn ʿArabī claimed. He furthermore taught that the spiritual perception of minerals is superior to that of humans. Hence, every mineral has unrestricted access to knowledge of the Unseen, which is only available to God's messengers, friends and sorcerers among humans.[127] Their knowledge of the Unseen does not automatically prevent minerals from being infidels (*kāfirūn*), disobedient (*ʿāṣ*) or hypocrites (*munāfiqūn*). Yet one would be hard pressed to find references to malevolent stones and metals in Ibn ʿArabī's works.[128] The scarcity of references mirrors the order of nature in this case: renegades, hypocrites and heretics constitute a small minority in the kingdom of minerals. Of all His creatures, Ibn ʿArabī maintained, minerals are the most obedient to God by far. The kingdom of minerals is untroubled by lust, ambition and heresy. Stones and metals have no presumptions to greatness either. They scarcely have any sense of self-awareness, and it is clouded by the realization that God is the only true judge presiding over things and events, past and present.[129] Every stone knows the exact reason why God brought it into existence nonetheless (e.g. to shatter the head of Goliath). Most humans are indifferent to common stones and metals: gone are the days when Bedouins bowed to stone blocks and mountains. In *al-Futūḥāt*, Ibn ʿArabī noted an attentive eye can be easily swayed by the greatness of mountains and boulders in terms of quantity (*kammiyya*) and mass (*jirm*). Although this is but a reflection of God's greatness, it prompted Bedouins to prostrate themselves before mountains in error. Then came Muhammad,

[126] Ibn ʿArabī, *K. al-maʿarif*, pp. 255–256; FM.II: 682.

[127] FM.II: 78, 682 FM.IV: 449. Ibn ʿArabī criticism of those who thought that minerals have no knowledge of Islam could come across as hypocritical, given that he once described stones and metals as passive subjects of nature (*al-mafʿūl al-ṭabīʿyy*), who have no knowledge of the active participle (*fāʿil*) that is God – much like chairs have no knowledge of a craftsman who made them. FM.I: 94.

[128] For instance, see FM.I: 209 and Chittick (trans.), 'Ibn ʿArabī's own Summary of Fusūṣ', p. 42.

[129] In his commentary on Ibn ʿArabī's book *Fuṣūṣ al-ḥikam*, Bosnevi (d. 1644) explained that minerals represent the symbol of absolute devotion to God, where no trace of the Self remains. He therefore advised spiritual seekers to pledge some gold to God, as no other sacrifice is as dear to Him. Bosnevi, *Sharḥ Fuṣūs al-ḥikam*, vol. 2, pp. 397–398.

spreading the message that God is one. Although no mineral is worth being worshiped, the Qur'an underscores the importance of showing them due respect, since 'the creation of the heavens and earth is greater than the creation of mankind, albeit most people know it not' (Q. 40:57). Ibn ʿArabī sought to rectify the ignorance of his readers by informing them that minerals are the purest, most pious creatures in existence.[130] The very word *islām* means 'submission to divine will' in Arabic. Based on this, Ibn ʿArabī reasoned that the obedience of minerals to God and His prophets allows for them to be recognized as Muslims. He furthermore argued that some minerals, such as the Black Stone at the eastern corner of the Kaaba for example, proved themselves better Muslims than certain humans![131]

Stones and metals do not adhere to the five pillars of Islam, however. Muhammad imposed different rules of conduct upon minerals, when he brought them the divine message (*al-risālat al-ilāhiyya*). The prophet knew as well as anyone that no mineral could travel to Mecca or prostrate itself on the ground in prayer. The corporeal form of minerals prevents them from doing so, which necessitated special laws and provisions to be made for them. Hence, Ibn ʿArabī explained, there is one Sharia for humans and another for minerals.

> When a solid substance undergoes dissolution, its form changes. Different forms call for different names to be made for them, and different laws as well. For instance, when a liquid solidifies and its form changes, we will refer to it [as ice instead of water] and different laws apply to it. Divine laws were revealed to living beings, taking into account their states, forms, and names. The essence of a living being has no direct ruling addressing it from its inherent nature. Things are judged as permissible (*mubāh*), obligatory (*wājib*), recommended (*mandūb*), forbidden (*maḥzūr*) or disliked (*makrūh*), depending on external circumstances and strange occurrences within the essences of things. Links and associations between earthly creatures and (im)pure spiritual entities play a role as well. A living being will struggle against its own nature, and demonic and angelic spirits besides, depending on the spiritual decrees and religious laws it follows.[132]

[130] FM.I: 710. See also FM.II: 105, 475, 612, FM.III: 2 and Ibn ʿArabī, *K. al-maʿarif*, p. 311. God does not hold minerals responsible for humans turning polytheist, Ibn ʿArabī maintained. Ibn ʿArabī, *K. al-Qasam al-ilāhī*, p. 174.

[131] FM.II: 622.

[132] FM.III: 390. The term '*adab*' served to denote appropriate, lawful conduct, culture and etiquette in Ibn ʿArabī's works. Again, minerals have their own version of *adab*. FM.II: 105, 202, 481. See also Abdel-hadi, *Ibn ʿArabī's Religious Pluralism*, p. 23.

In other words, a mineral may be considered a good Muslim even if it does not obey the religious laws governing human conduct. The spiritual aspirations of minerals also differ from those of humans. For instance, no stone dreams of ascending through the seven heavens. Minerals do not seek to rise above others and grow towards the Sun like plants. Dragging a stone upwards by force or throwing it towards the heavens would not be appreciated by the stone itself and it would throw itself back to the ground deliberately, shrinking in fear of God – this is how Ibn ʿArabī interpreted the seventy-fourth verse of the surah *al-Baqarah* (Q. 2:74). He believed it is fear, rather than gravitation, that causes stones to fall back to earth. 'Verily, we take a stone', Ibn ʿArabī said, 'whose nature is to fall and throw it into the air. Ascent does not come naturally to a stone. It is a miracle comparable to the spiritual ascension of humans, which also goes against the laws of nature.'[133]

To summarize, piety and virtue are the main character traits of (almost) all inhabitants of the mineral kingdom. Every mineral has access to the knowledge of the Unseen, which is not the case with humans. They are exemplary believers, untouched by all the sins that cause the human heart to darken and rust. Some minerals are less perfect than others nonetheless, which is evident when contrasting the coarse appearance of iron and the radiance of gold. That brings us to the following questions:

- What is the source of corruption in the kingdom of minerals?
- What makes some minerals less perfect than others?
- Since minerals cannot sin, why aren't we surrounded with heaps and mountains of gold?
- How can alchemists support the spiritual practices of minerals seeking to turn themselves into gold?

God is not directly responsible for corruption among minerals, Ibn ʿArabī maintained. The Creator does not favour one mineral over another, and He maintains no special relationship with any of them. One must turn to Mother Nature to uncover the causes of mineral corruption. My Element will demonstrate that Ibn ʿArabī believed there is a direct link between spiritual and bodily health. Although mineral spirits are inherently pure, forces of nature cause their bodies to sicken at birth (or later) – which leads to the corruption of the spirit. Ibn ʿArabī said: 'Minerals are divided into step-levels of spiritual excellence (*marātib*) based

[133] Ibn ʿArabī, *K. Manzil al-manāzil*, p. 186.

on what happened to them when they were created, when their organic bodies were first formed.'[134] An alchemist's task is to comprehend the genesis of minerals, so as to be able to identify (and eliminate) the corruptive influences hindering the transmutation of iron into gold. To gain this knowledge, alchemists were advised to visit the Sphere of Saturn, which is the seventh heaven.[135] For those of us with no access to higher heavens, Ibn ʿArabī's works will suffice. Chapter 167 of his book *al-Futūḥāt* contains the following information:

> The first action and the first gift to be received at the seventh heaven, at that starry sphere, is how iron turns into silver through careful manipulation and craftmanship, and how iron turns into gold by refining its properties – which is a wonderful secret indeed! This knowledge is not sought after for the sake of abundance in wealth, but for the pursuit of abundant excellence, to attain the rank of perfection and acquire in its composition the first rank of metallic vapours through astronomical movements and natural heat, mercury and sulphur, and each substance in a metal seeks the ultimate goal, which is perfection, and we refer to this perfection as 'gold'. But alas, flaws and diseases arise in a metal, such as excessive dryness or excessive moisture, heat or cold, which disturb its balance, and this illness affects the form (*ṣūra*) of a metal, which is then referred to as 'iron', 'copper', 'brass' and the like.[136]

This is a dense paragraph, saturated with information, with quite a few things to unpack. Together, we will dissect it gradually, and with caution. There is a long way ahead of iron yearning to turn itself into gold – that much is clear. The quoted paragraph, however, clarifies that the word 'gold' represents the perfect bodily health and appearance of minerals, as well as the highest spiritual rank a mineral can reach. Health and rank could be gained by iron simultaneously if it were to refine its bodily constitution (*takwīn*), for the health of the body leads to spiritual health. Three factors were identified in the text as the causes of corruption among minerals:

1. Metallic vapours stirred by celestial spheres and natural heat
2. Mercury and sulphur
3. Excessive dryness, moisture, heat and/or cold.

[134] FM.II: 272. See also FM.I: 365–366. Although minerals are corrupted at birth in most cases, my Element will demonstrate that Ibn ʿArabī believed extant gold is also not immune to corruption.

[135] FM.I: 152. FM.II: 420–421. Elsewhere, Ibn ʿArabī linked this knowledge with the Sphere of the Sun and Idris/Hermes. FM.I: 155.

[136] FM.I: 152.

Elsewhere, two other factors were identified: the exact time and place where iron stepped into existence.[137] Each of these factors comes into play during the creation process of minerals, and iron must undo the damage it caused to acquire the perfection of gold. Now, the immediate goal is to pinpoint the impacts that the five factors have on mineral bodies. We will then use this information to establish a provisional hierarchy of stones and metals in Ibn ᶜArabī's works. The shaykh thought this knowledge a prerequisite for undertaking a successful alchemical transmutation, which will be analysed in Section 6.

We have already seen that Ibn ᶜArabī regarded the genesis of minerals and the workings of alchemical transmutation as facets of the same knowledge. His understanding of the act of genesis bears resemblance to the writings of Aristotle and Jābir. Namely, Aristotle believed that minerals are formed by subterranean winds and vapours arising from volcanic heat and earthquakes. This is the first factor governing the generation and corruption of minerals Ibn ᶜArabī identified. Smoky, dry vapours produce minerals such as sulphur, which do not melt when exposed to heat. Moist vapours, however, create fusible stones and metals such as mercury.[138] 'Sulphur' and 'mercury' served as synonyms for dry and moist vapours, respectively, in the Jabirian corpus. Not only was Jābir b. Hayyān identified as the father of Islamic alchemy, but he was also traditionally perceived as the inventor of sulphur–mercury theory, which was influential among the early modern and medieval alchemists, Christians and Muslims alike. The gist of this theory is that all minerals are made of sulphur and mercury,[139] which were symbolically depicted as two birds, the Sun and the Moon, and/or mother and father in alchemical writings.[140]

137 FM.I: 365–366. The spiritual and bodily health of nearby humans can also play a role in the spiritual development of minerals once in a while. This is the topic for another section (Section 7).

138 See Aristotle, *Meteorologica*, pp. 290–377; Holmyard-Russel (eds.), *The Works of Geber*, p. xi; Norris, 'The Mineral Exaltations', pp. 43–65 and Emerton, *The Scientific Reinterpretation of Form*, p. 23. This was the predominant view on the origins of minerals in Europe until the seventeenth century, with Dym demonstrating it influenced prospectors, investors and mining officials alike. Dym, 'Alchemy and Mining', pp. 232–233. See also Linden, *The Alchemy Reader*, p. 13.

139 An in-depth analysis of (Pseudo-)Jābir's views on the topic can be found at Haq, *Names, Natures and Things*, p. 46; Levey, 'Arabic Mineralogy of the Tenth Century', p. 21; Stapleton, 'The Sayings Attributed to Hermes', p. 81; Zirnis, 'The Kitāb Usṭuqus al-Uss', pp. 14–15. Here it should be noted that Homlyard and Russel argued that 'mother' and 'father' Jābir was referring to are not really mercury and sulphur, 'but hypothetical substances to which ordinary sulphur and mercury form the closest available approximations'. Holmyard-Russel (eds.), *The Works of Geber*, p. xiii.

140 Examples of how alchemical marriage – or the first mixture (*al-mizāj al-awwal*) – was depicted in Islamic art can be found at Müller, 'The Alchemical Symbols in the Manuscripts of "The Mirror of Wonders" (Mirāt al-ᶜajāʾib)', pp. 702–703.

There are works attributed to Jābir suggesting one could extract sulphur and mercury from every stone and metal. For centuries, these works served as an inspiration for alchemists trying to get their hands on pure extracts of mercury and sulphur. These extracts were sometimes identified with red sulphur and/or philosopher's stone on the authority of Jābir, which alchemists hoped to use to turn common stones and metals into gold. Herman Boerhaave (d. 1738), for instance, kept mercury at the steady temperature of 100 degrees Celsius for over fifteen years, until his assistant spilled it by accident. George Starkey (d. 1665) chose to work with antimony instead, treating it with strong acids and saltpetre in hope of extracting pure sulphur from it.[141] Pseudo-Zosimos conducted similar experiments with mercury, magnesia and cinnabar, with the Jabirian corpus suggesting an alchemist would also get good results by working with arsenic, sal ammoniac, vinegar and silver.[142] There are no surviving records of comparable experiments Ibn ʿArabī may have performed.

Angela Jaffray documented that Ibn ʿArabī had more than a passing knowledge of the Jabirian corpus.[143] Among other things, he recognized mercury (*ziʾbaq*) and sulphur (*kibrīt*) as the mother and father of all minerals in *al-Futūḥāt*. Ibn ʿArabī furthermore clarified that he coined the term 'the kingdom of minerals' because all stones and metals were born (*tawallud*) from a mother and father.[144] Gold is the perfect child of mercury and sulphur, whose birth necessitates that both mother and father are balanced out, healthy and evenly exposed to sustained heat.[145] Here it ought to be reiterated that heat is one of the factors governing the generation and corruption of minerals, which Ibn ʿArabī mentioned in chapter 167 of *al-Futūḥāt.* The conjugal union of Father Sulphur and Mother Mercury is another factor he identified.

141 Holmyard-Russel (eds.), *The Works of Geber*, pp. 3–5. See also: Bacon, *The Mirror of Alchemy*, p. 2; Newman-Principe, *Alchemy Tried in Fire*, p. 101; Hughes, *The Rise of Alchemy*, pp. 44–45; Roberts, 'Rectifying the Pharaoh', p. 25; Taslimi, 'An Examination of "'Nihāyat al-ṭalab"', p. 54; Marlow Taylor, *The Alchemy of al-Razi*, p. 68, Stapleton-Taylor, 'The Sayings of Hermes', p. 82 and Zirnis, 'The Kitāb Usṭuqus al-Uss', p. 42.

142 For instance, see Petrus Bonus, *The New Pearl of Great Price*, pp. 311–312; Zosimos, *Muṣḥaf al-ṣuwar*, p. 373 and Zirnis, 'The Kitāb Usṭuqus al-Uss', pp. 56–59.

143 Ibn ʿArabī, *K. al-Isfār*, pp. 228–229.

144 FM.I: 583; FM.II: 105. Kant once said even a band of devils could found a state, 'provided they have only the necessary intelligence'. Hallaq, *The Impossible State*, p. 19. Borders between the kingdoms of minerals, humans, plants and animals in Ibn ʿArabī's works could be porous at times; for instance, Ibn ʿArabī argued that the lowliest inhabitant of each of these kingdoms is a citizen of a neighboring kingdom. 'The last of the minerals and the first of plants is truffle,' he said. 'The last of plants and the first of animals is the palm tree. The last of animals and the first of humans is the monkey.' Ibn ʿArabī, *ʿUqlat al-mustawfiz*, p. 124. Cf. FM.I: 593–594.

145 FM.I: 592–593; FM.II: 270–271.

Now, Section 2 declared my Element will not dwell on metaphors. An exception needs to be made here, however, since the terms 'mercury' and 'sulphur', 'mother' and 'father', had a broader meaning in Akbarian context. 'Mother' and 'father' were synonyms for active and passive principles – the movers and the moved – in Ibn ʿArabī's works. 'Father sulphur' thus represents the divine spirit sculpting mother nature, which is ever-changing and 'mercurial'. Ibn ʿArabī believed that the universe and all in it originate from a single soul and essence, which is God, and he cited from the Qur'an in support of his teachings (Q. 4:1, 15:29). 'God's spirit turns to face the essentials,' Ibn ʿArabī recorded, 'and these essentials are the components accepting alternation and transformation'.[146] The essentials he was referring to are fire, water, air and earth. These four elements are the building blocks of the universe, and each of them partakes in the formation of mineral bodies.[147] The 'sulphuric' revolution of the heavenly spheres spins these elements, which causes them to turn into stones and metals. Celestial spheres, whose revolution produces the four elements, as well as hot, cold, dry and/or moist climate on Earth are the third factor dictating the genesis of minerals, which Ibn ʿArabī described in chapter 167 of *al-Futūḥāt.*

The impact of the Moon on tides has been known for millennia. Once, the Moon was closer to Earth and tides were stronger, which may have forced bony fish to emerge onto land and develop limbs over time according to Peter Frankopan.[148] Ibn ʿArabī thought that celestial bodies such as the Moon float passively within the heavenly spheres. The revolution of spheres causes stars and planets to revolve around Earth. Akbarians also believed that celestial bodies and spheres influence the growth, state and health of living beings on Earth.[149] The full extent of their influence was not known to many people. Authorities on the subject were collectively referred to as the Community of the Scale (*ummah al-mizān*) in Ibn ʿArabī's works. He spoke dismissively of this group of scholars, whom he found materialistic and unconcerned with the Divine. He respected their knowledge, however,[150] and he shared some of it in *al-Futūḥāt* and elsewhere.

[146] FM.I: 138–139. Cf. FM.I: 583, 691; FM.II: 272, 460 and Ibn ʿArabī, *K. al-maʿarif*, p. 244.

[147] Although humans tend to identify minerals with the element of earth, every corporeal form contains all four elements. The proof of this, Ibn ʿArabī said, is that flint can be used to make fire. FM.III: 396.

[148] Frankopan, *The Earth Transformed*, p. 28.

[149] FM.I: 394, 514; Ibn ʿArabī, K. *Shaqq al-jayb*, p. 317.

[150] Alchemy was also known as the Science of the Scale (*ʿilm al-mizān*) in Islam. Ibn ʿArabī used this term in *al-Futūḥāt* at times (e.g. FM.I: 161), for reasons that will become clear by the end of this section.

Once again, I invite the reader to consult Figure 1 depicting the planetary spheres. These seven spheres, and the celestial bodies they carry, play the key role in the creation of minerals – with the help of the stars from the lunar mansion *Saᶜd al-dhābiḥ*, in the Capricorn constellation.[151] There are another 254 spheres and orbits Ibn ᶜArabī described, however, which *also* play a role in the act of genesis. Ibn ᶜArabī collectively described them as 'raised ceilings above Earth' and 'layers of onion'. The planet Earth sits at the centre of this cosmic onion, whose layers are glued to one another.[152] The movements of planetary spheres thus impact the orbit of fire, water and air, which are situated directly above Earth and below the planetary spheres (Figure 3).

The four elements and mineral bodies alike are formed by the rotation of heavenly orbits and spheres. There is something sexual about the way they revolve around Earth, Ibn ᶜArabī said. As they spin, spheres bring the following qualities into existence: wetness, dryness, coldness and heat. 'Hot and dry quality then mix to create fire. Hot and wet create air. Cold and wet create water, and cold and dry quality create the element of earth.'[153] Now, *how* exactly mineral bodies and elements emerge from the spinning orbits and spheres was never clarified in Ibn ᶜArabī's oeuvre. He described this process evasively as 'a strange mystery and difficult complexity which is forbidden to be revealed since it cannot be borne and the intellect couldn't take it'.[154] One thing is certain, however: Ibn ᶜArabī believed that the orbits depicted in Figure 3 could force elements which would not normally interact with one another (e.g. fire and earth) to come to together against their will. This causes the corporeal forms of minerals, plants, animals and humans to emerge (somehow). Higher spheres and orbits – with the orbit of fire being the highest elemental orbit in existence – rule the orbits below. Were the impact of a higher sphere to become exceedingly strong, the disbalance of elements would occur,[155] causing sickness and corruption to appear on Earth.

Mens sana in corpore sano, the Ancient Romans used to say – a sound mind in a sound body. Ibn ᶜArabī likewise taught that the body causes the mind and soul to rot – with curly hair, blue eyes and skinny bodies

---

151 FM.II 460–461.

152 See Rašić, *The Written World of God*, p. 150. There are no surviving diagrams in Ibn ᶜArabī's hand depicting the exact location of each of the 261 orbits he mentioned. All we know is he believed them to revolve around the Earth.

153 FM.I: 55, 142.

154 FM.I: 55–56. An attempt to get to the bottom of this mystery can be found at Rašić, 'Celestial Mechanics', pp. 65–87.

155 FM.I: 142; FM.II: 457.

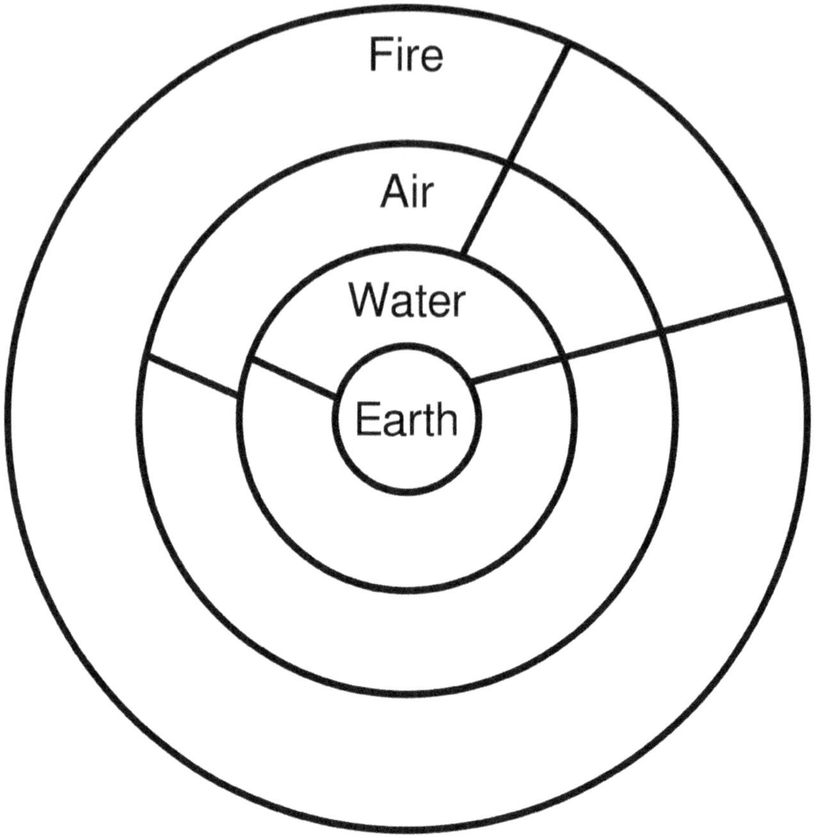

Figure 3 Elemental orbits. Drawing by the author based on Ibn ʿArabī's *Kitāb ʿUqlat al-mustawfiz* (MS Yusuf Aga 4690, ff. 11. Konya: Yusuf Aga Library, 617 AH).

indicating a human is plagued by disbalances of elements. The same disbalances cause lesser stones and metals to be born to Father Sulphur and Mother Mercury.[156] Extant gold, however pristine, is not impervious to sickness and decay either. The power of perfection (*quwwa al-kamāl*) that gold possesses, Ibn ʿArabī claimed, cannot protect it from the corrupt influences of heavenly bodies and spheres. This is where alchemists could step in to help. A skilled alchemist can evaluate disbalances at a glance. 'Their craft is called alchemy,' Ibn ʿArabī explained, 'which is nothing but

[156] FM.I: 275; FM.II: 235–236, FM.IV: 279. Ibn ʿArabī, like al-ʿIrāqī, thought that coldness in nature causes gold to become silver. FM.I: 592–593. Al-ʿIrāqī furthermore clarified that too much dryness would cause it to become marcasite or magnesia instead. He also said that excessive moisture leads to the birth of mercury. Al-ʿIrāqī, *The Book of Knowledge*, p. 14.

the knowledge of measures (*maqādīr*) and weights (*awzān*)'.[157] Alchemy consequently came to be known as the Science of the Scale (*ᶜilm al-mizān*) in Muslim cultures and societies.

> Sages oversee and manage their patients, and they can look at the heart of the matter. The easiest and the best way for them to proceed is to remove defects from mineral bodies by observing celestial bodies swimming in their orbits, through the mansions of the Moon – one moment inside a mansion, then swerving away, above and below. A sage always knows what caused their patient to become iron instead [of gold].[158]

Alchemists sometimes use the light of the Sun and the Moon – as well as the light of Mercury, Venus, Mars, Jupiter and Saturn – to assist them in their craft. The lights of the seven spheres also play a role in the creation of mineral bodies. The nature and properties of these lights change with every hour, day and season of the year. The light of the Moon shines the brightest on Monday, for instance. An alchemist will undertake their operations on Monday should the Moon be identified as the source of corruption they wish to reverse. They would be wise to operate on Sunday, however, if corruption stems from the Sun (further details on the exact correspondences between celestial spheres and days of the week can be found in Table 1, towards the end of this section). Another thing to be considered is that minerals created in spring have different properties from those born in winter. Climate conditions – hot summers, cold winters, dry autumns and moist springs – play a major role in the generation and corruption of minerals. Ibn ᶜArabī taught that 'every season of the year has a specific impact on the substance of created things and elements – causing them to become thinned out or thickened, cooled or heated, moisturized or dried out'.[159] In short, climate conditions set the stage for the intercourse between Father Sulphur and Mother Mercury.

The generation of minerals, Ibn ᶜArabī explained, is not unlike the birth of a human child, whose disposition is immaculate and pure at birth – before their parents raise them as Christian, Magi or Jewish. Climate conditions prevent Father Sulphur and Mother Mercury regularly from making gold, and they can also corrupt healthy children in time. Malformed minerals

[157] FM.I: 152.

[158] FM.II: 271. Ibn ᶜArabī linked the sages who can recognize and (re)establish the perfection of minerals with the dwellers of Arin, which is the is the heavenly citadel located Ibn ᶜArabī saw in his visions of paradise. A drawing of this citadel in Ibn ᶜArabī's hand survives, and it can be consulted at Ibn ᶜArabī, *al-Futūḥāt al-Makkiyya* (MS YAZMA 1870), ff. 94 and Rašić, *The Written World of God*, p. 48. See also FM.II: 129.

[159] FM.II: 460. See also FM.I: 365–366 and FM.II: 270.

pass on their corruption to plants, which are then consumed by animals (and humans).[160] Ibn ᶜArabī thought that the most noble creatures in existence dwell around Mecca, which is ruled by the fourth clime. Given there are seven planetary spheres and the seven lights governing the seasons of the year,[161] it is only proper there are seven climes as well.

Ancient Greeks and Romans recognized the existence of seven climes and discussed their impact on the character and appearance of living beings centuries before Ibn ᶜArabī.[162] They believed that the cold weather of northern Europe, which is ruled by the first climate, breeds men who are unintelligent and brave. Further south, marshes breed sickness and make Gaul prone to savagery, superstition and insurrection. Seasoned generals such as Gnaeus Domitius Corbulo dreaded being ordered to take charge of Roman garrisons in Antioch, for it was once common knowledge that the warm weather of Syria turns men soft.[163] Alchemists concerned themselves with the provenance of minerals because the seven climes were thought to have an impact on the core (*jawhar*), state and appearance of minerals. Climes have the same effect on the ecosystem as a whole, simultaneously uplifting or debasing minerals, plants, humans and animals. This is also what Ibn ᶜArabī believed.[164] Now, there were several notable attempts in contemporary scholarship to determine the exact coordinates on the map where each of the seven climes rules. I will not recount them here since as early as the eleventh century, al-Bīrūnī (d. 1050) mockingly noted one could hardly find two manuscripts with identical coordinates.[165] There was a general consensus among scholars, however, that the most brilliant and pious men are born and raised under the favourable conditions of the fourth clime, which ruled the central section of antique maps and globes.

160 FM.I: 209; FM.II: 270–271.

161 Ibn ᶜArabī believed that celestial spheres govern the passing of hours, days, and seasons of the year. FM.II: 282.

162 The exact origin of these theories, which were transmitted to Muslim cultures and societies through Graeco-Arabic translation movement and the works of Ptolemy, Galen and Hippocrates, remains unclear. See Olsson, 'The World in the Arab Eyes', p. 488.

163 Holland, *Pax*, p.83.

164 FM.II: 270–271.

165 The reason for this being that every scholar sought to demonstrate that they themselves were born under the favorable influences of the fourth clime. So, the fourth clime was said to rule over North Africa, Sicily, Basra, Kufa, Baghdad, Wasit and Mesopotamia – as well as Samarqand, Bukhara, Nishapur, Isfahan, Syria, Morocco and Spain, depending on where the aspiring climatologist was born. Al-Bīrūnī, *K. Taḥdid al-amākin*, pp. 100–101. Contemporary attempts to map out the regions under the influences of the seven climes can be consulted at Al-Azmeh, 'Barbarians in the Arab Eyes', p. 6; Harvey, 'A New Islamic Source of the *Guide of the Perplexed*', 36–41 and Olsson, 'The World in the Arab Eyes', pp. 493–495.

On his side, Ibn ᶜArabī believed that the fourth clime rules over Mecca, Madina and Sinai. 'Whatever we discover, the reality (*wujūd*) of it will be more radiant and perfect in Mecca,' he said.

> Like spiritual stations have different ranks, places on Earth also differ in excellence. Likewise, no stone could compete with pearl – except in the eyes of a person with no spiritual discernment. A person of rank – a cultivated person – can differentiate between them as God would. God himself does not equate a house made of mudbrick and straw with a house built of gold and silver bricks … The most noble angels and righteous jinn gather around Mecca, which is also imbued with *himma* of every human who once lived there.[166]

Ibn ᶜArabī hoped his writings would prompt neophytes to visit Mecca, since the city clime could do wonders for the spiritual development and practices of both humans and minerals. Mecca is also the ideal place to search for red sulphur (the topic discussed in Section 7).

So, in the ideal case, a mineral would be born in Mecca and nurtured by the warmth of the fourth clime. Whether the birth itself took on fertile soil, within a stony mountain or in the depths of the Red Sea was of no importance to Ibn ᶜArabī, as long as a newborn mineral was exposed to sustained heat from the start.[167] The birth of gold would be ensured if Father Sulphur – which stands for the planetary spheres and the seven lights they spin – were to be brought into equilibrium with the four elements representing Mother Mercury. Alas, more often than not the disbalances resulting from the complex interplay between the four elements, the seven lights and the revolution of celestial spheres cause mineral bodies to decay. The severity of their bodily decay determines the hierarchy of minerals, which we will now seek to outline.

The highest step-level in Ibn ᶜArabī's hierarchy of minerals belongs to gold – that much was clear from the start. Gold is the only metal which was spared from suffering the negative influences of the elements, climes and spheres. The second place in the hierarchy belongs to silver, which is short of gold-like perfection by one degree only (*daraja wahḍa*).[168] 'As of other

166 FM.I: 99; FM.II: 105. Ibn ᶜArabī curiously noted that Madina was once an impure place, infested with fever. The prophet Muhammad prayed to God to cleanse the city once he saw it caused his father-in-law, Abū Bakr, and Bilal b. Rabāḥ to fall ill. Thereafter, air-borne sicknesses plagued Medina no more. God had them removed 'like fire removes impurity from silver'. FM.I: 758.

167 Brethren of Purity conversely believed that minerals which were formed in fertile soil would ripen faster than those that were formed in interiors of other stones. Brethren of Purity, *On the Natural Sciences*, p. 230, 267–269.

168 FM.I: 592–593.

mineral forms', Ibn ʿArabī said, 'they contain illnesses and defects leading them astray from the path of perfection – and thus we have mercury, lead, tin, iron, copper and silver'.[169] Ibn ʿArabī exhibited the tendency to let others dwell on decay and corruption: his preferred topic was the nature of perfection. Thus, it remains unclear which mineral he deemed the basest. Chapter 198 of *al-Futūḥāt*, however, clarified he regarded sapphire as a mid-tier substance, ranked between the basest of minerals and gold.[170] Table 1 represents an attempt to make a top-list of minerals of a sort, based on presumed links and correspondences between God's prophets, climes and minerals Ibn Arabi established in *al-Futūḥāt al-Makkiyya* and *K. al-Tadbīrāt al-ilāhiyya*.

Five centuries later, Hegel contested analogous schemes linking planets to metals. It is completely natural and logical that someone would compare the Sun to gold and the Moon to silver, he said, although 'planets do not belong to the same field as metals and the chemical process'.[171] Ibn ʿArabī might have responded to Hegel's criticism with a characteristically indifferent shrug, had he had a chance to read his arguments. For he was adamant that his knowledge is a product of the divine visions and unveilings he received, and he claimed God revealed to him that He entrusted each of His prophets with a precious stone or metal.[172] In Section 4 we saw there are seven prophets presiding over the seven planetary spheres.

Each of these prophets has a secret or two to share on alchemy (again, see Section 4). According to Ibn ʿArabī, minerals that were entrusted to God's prophets have special properties as well. For instance, emeralds make it easier for Sufis to practise *dhikr*, which is the act of remembrance of God. They also protect humans from Iblis the Devil, with Ibn ʿArabī claiming emeralds can blind evil spirits and alert humans of their presence. Rubies can calm fears and anger and reveal secrets of the divine essence (*dhāt al-Ḥaqq*). As of sapphires, the blue ones were said to carry the power to turn an ordinary person into a great leader. A yellow sapphire, however, will endow its owner with the markings of servitude (*ʿubūdīyya*), humility (*dhull*) and repute (*iftikār*).[173]

[169] FM.II: 460.

[170] Ibn ʿArabī said: 'Sapphire is a stage of development between a mineral and gold. When a mineral reaches this step-level, its form (*ṣūra*) will change visibly and it will begin turning into gold.' FM.II: 420-1.

[171] Quoted according to Magee, *Hegel and the Hermetic Tradition*, p. 195.

[172] FM.I: 5.

[173] Ibn ʿArabī, *K. al-Tadbīrāt al-ilāhiyya*, pp. 390–393. Ibn ʿArabī regarded the familiarity with special traits and properties of stones and metals as a noble knowledge and one of

Table 1 Correspondences between the heavenly spheres, precious stones and metals, climes, prophets and days of the week in Akbarian Sufism

	Celestial sphere	Prophet	Mineral	Clime	Day of the week
1	Saturn, the seventh heaven	Abraham	?	first	Saturday
2	Jupiter, the sixth heaven	Moses	Sapphire	second	Thursday
3	Mars, the fifth heaven	Aaron & David	Red gold	third	Tuesday
4	Sun, the fourth heaven	Idris	?	fourth	Sunday
5	Venus, the third heaven	Joseph	Yellow gold	fifth	Friday
6	Mercury, the second heaven	Jesus & Yahya	Ruby	sixth	Wednesday
7	Moon, the lowest heaven	Adam	Emerald	seventh	Monday

There are seven important minerals, Ibn ʿArabī said, corresponding to the seven heavens and the seven days of the week.[174] Now, Ibn ʿArabī believed that the purity of living beings, forms and objects increases progressively with their distance from Earth.[175] By this logic, one could easily reach the conclusion that God would entrust Abraham with gold since this prophet presides over the highest planetary sphere in existence. Table 1, however, demonstrates this was not the case.[176] It lists the seven heavens in descending order, from highest to lowest:

Red sulphur was linked with the Perfect Human being in Ibn ʿArabī's works. The model of human excellence in Akbarian circles was the prophet Muhammad, who is not featured in Table 1. Ibn ʿArabī did not specify which mineral God chose for Muhammad – was it red sulphur or something else entirely? – nor did he elaborate on potential correspondences between red sulphur and celestial spheres. Another thing he failed to mention is which stones were chosen for Idris/Hermes and Abraham. I believe these omissions to be intentional.

the prerogatives of the Sufi Pole (al-Quṭb, the Pole, is the title of the most accomplished spiritual practitioner among the living humans in Sufi literature). One could try to gain access to this knowledge by engaging in *dhikr*. See Ibn ʿArabī, *K. al-Quṭb wal-imāmayn*, p. 219 and Ibn ʿArabī, *Risāla al-anwār*, p. 156.

174 FM.II: 460–461.

175 Like clearest water can be found at the top of the jug, with residue at the bottom, the purest things in existence live at a distance far away from Earth. FM.I: 154.

176 Table 1 is based on the information provided in FM.I: 5, 154–156 and Ibn ʿArabī, *K. al-Tadbīrāt al-ilāhiyya*, pp. 390–393. There are comparable lists in Mesopotamian and Greek sources Karpenko analysed, where the central place on the list was also reserved for gold. See Karpenko, 'Systems of Metals', p. 208, 216–217.

Climes, rather than spheres, served as the basis for Ibn ʿArabī's hierarchy of precious stones and metals in Table 1. This is evident at a glance: gold occupies the central rows of Table 1, like the fourth clime rules the central portions of antique maps. Now, chapter 15 of *al-Futūḥāt* established links between the seven climes and planetary spheres.[177] These were also documented in Table 1, which reveals that the best of climes does *not* correspond to the highest of spheres. When speaking to Ibn ʿArabī, God linked the Sphere of Saturn with the first clime, whose impact on living beings is horrendous. At no point did Ibn ʿArabī address this paradox in his works, nor did he explain why God did not entrust gold to Hermes, who is the ruler of the fourth clime, which is the best of the seven. Yellow gold and red gold were linked with the prophets presiding over the third and the fifth clime instead. It was probably easier for Ibn ʿArabī to omit the information on red sulphur, Muhammad, and the stone of Abraham and Hermes than to probe God's knowledge for inconsistencies.

Here, I would suggest a potential explanation for His linking red and yellow gold to the third and the fifth clime, based on chapter 15 of *al-Futūḥāt.* In this chapter, Ibn ʿArabī mentions the existence of seven spiritual seekers he referred to as 'Abdāl'. The word *abdāl* means 'substitute' in Arabic. The seven Abdāls Ibn ʿArabī described follow in the footsteps of God's prophets and serve as their substitutes. There are seven Abdāls at any given point of time, Ibn ʿArabī said, and they preside over the seven climes. Through these people, God sustains existence on Earth and the moment one of them dies, He will appoint another person to serve in their place.[178] Ibn ʿArabī claimed to have personally met with the Abdāl who were active in his lifetime.[179] They informed him that every Abdāl can draw power from their prophet – or rather, from a celestial body that floats in the sphere which is presided by the prophet in whose footsteps they follow. So, the Abdāl presiding over the third clime draws their power from Mars, and the one in charge of the fifth clime wields the might of Venus. However, Abdāls also revealed to Ibn ʿArabī that those in charge of the fifth and the third clime are *also* supported by Muhammad himself. Since the prophet Muhammad is the epitome of human perfection, it is only proper for these Abdāls to be linked with the perfect mineral – gold.[180] Whereas divine intentions between the great order of things might be unclear, Muhammad's inference and the seven climes are clearly the

177 FM.I: 154–156.
178 FM.I: 4; FM.II: 7.
179 FM.II: 7.
180 FM.II: 455.

deciding factors behind the hierarchy of minerals in Table 1. With this knowledge, we can proceed to Section 6 and discuss the transmutation of lesser stones and metals into gold.

6 Mineral Magic: (Extra)ordinary Transmutations

The sixth section of my Element will determine what constitutes a successful alchemical transmutation according to the criteria Ibn ʿArabī established. This requires us to pinpoint his definition of the form (*ṣūra*), root (*aṣl*), essence (*ʿayn*) and substance of minerals (*jawhar*): only then will it be possible to understand the ontological principles governing the transmutation of iron into gold. Ibn ʿArabī affirmed the reality of alchemical transmutations, on the authority of God himself. Not everyone shared this opinion.

The royal art has been traditionally linked with sages, as well as swindlers. The imperial edicts cited in Section 4, which are the earliest surviving records on alchemy worldwide, reveal that the Han court of China made a distinction between gold metal, legally mined, and the counterfeit gold of alchemists. Graeco-Egyptian treatises – such as the Leyden Papyrus X, for example – also speak of a gold-like alloy so perfect 'it will deceive even an expert'.[181] The seventh-century historian John of Antioch purported that the emperor Diocletian banned and burned 290 works on alchemy because he feared Egyptians could use their surfeit, counterfeit gold to fund rebellions against Rome.[182] The second book of the Bible describes how God blessed Bezalel, son of Uri, with the ability to work with gold, silver, precious stones and bronze (Exodus 35: 30–35). Yet Christian tradition linked metallurgy, goldsmithing and alchemy with fallen angels, rather than God. Wicked angels taught these skills to their lovers when 'they fell from heaven upon the daughters of Eve and added fresh shame to womankind'.[183] The witch-hunting manual *Maleus Malleficarum*, however, maintained demons can only create an illusion of gold and that 'the authors of alchemy should be aware that one metal cannot be changed into another'.[184]

---

181 The treatise known as the *Leyden Papyrus X* was penned around the late third or the early fourth century in Greek. Images of the original document, as well as an English rendition of the text, can be found at Hopkins, *Alchemy*, p. 45, 247.

182 Kambylus (ed.), *Ioannis Antiocheni fragment aquae supersunt omnia*, p. 349.

183 For instance, see Tertullian, *De cultu feminarum*, pp. 714–715 and Winder (ed.), *The Complete Book of Enoch*, pp. 16–17. Further examples can be found at Bull, 'Wicked Angels and the Good Demon', p. 3, 5.

184 Kramer, *Malleus maleficarum*, p. 45.

Ḥunayn b. Isḥāq, al-Kindī, Ibn Rushd and Avicenna were among those who questioned the possibility of turning iron into gold in Muslim cultures and societies. Avicenna in particular noted how alchemists dye metals to make them resemble gold. Although their products could be mistaken for gold at times, they were in every way inferior to it.[185] Averroes and Ibn Khaldun were of the same opinion, favouring Mother Nature over synthetic products.[186] They likely feared that suggestions an alchemist could create real gold would expose them to accusations of disbelief (*kufr*) – for how could humans compare with God, the Creator? Yet this is precisely what the author(s) of the Jabirian and Hermetic corpus maintained, writing under pseudonyms, from behind the shield of anonymity: this made it possible for them to claim that humans *can* replicate Nature's handiworks perfectly. The fire caused by lightning and the one started by flint stone are essentially the same, Pseudo-Jabir claimed, although the latter is 'artificial' in its mode of production.[187] Ibn ᶜArabī adopted a more balanced view, seeking to reconcile the passion for alchemy with piety.

Although he thought it possible to turn iron into gold, Ibn ᶜArabī rarely passed over the opportunity to emphasize the superiority of God over humans. He piously claimed that raw gold in nature – being God's own work – exceeds the artistry of human goldsmiths.[188] Ibn ᶜArabī was also ready to admit there *are* illusionists and swindlers among alchemists. Some of them rely on sorcery and *himma* to confuse the human eye and mind, so that it would appear to them a sorcerer turned marble into gold. The Qur'an describes how Moses fell for a similar trick when sorcerers of the pharaoh made their sticks appear as if they were snakes (Q. 7:116). Such illusions constitute a lesser form of sorcery, Ibn ᶜArabī maintained, since Egyptian sorcerers did not cause the form and essence of their sticks to change.[189] A mighty sorcerer *could* temporarily change the corporeal form of a snake, however. As a matter of fact, God sometimes intervenes to help sorcerers with their tricks, when they wish to turn themselves

185 Avicenna, *De congelatione et conglutinatione lapidum*, pp. 17–45. It is therefore ironic that, over the course of centuries, works on alchemy have been attributed to Avicenna, as documented in Stapleton-Lewis, 'Two Alchemical Treatises Attributed to Avicenna', pp. 41–82. See also Hassan, *Studies in al-Kimiya'*, p. 62.

186 Ibn Rushd's views on alchemy survive in his commentary of Aristotle's book *Generation of Animals*. Averroes, *Aristotelis opera cum Averrois commentariis*, vol. 6, p. 44. Cf. Newman, *Promethean Ambitions*, p. 6 and Ibn Khaldūn, *al-Muqaddima*, vol. 3, pp. 227–246.

187 Newman (ed.), *The Summa Perfectionis of Pseudo-Geber*, pp. 11–12. Further information on *The Book of Hermes* (MS BN lat. 6514, ff.13) can be found at Newman, *Promethean Ambitions*, p. 64.

188 Ibn ᶜArabī, *Sḥarh tarjumān al-ashwāq*, p. 165.

189 FM.I: 235–236.

into a lion, rock or plant while retaining the human mind (it is a cunning strategy of His against disbelievers, Ibn ʿArabī said, although he did not elaborate on details).[190] The essence of what makes them human also remains untouched while sorcerers play at being lions. Eventually, magic ends and sorcerers return to their original form.

Here it should be noted that no human can fully turn themselves into a lion, because the human essence and lion essence (*ʿayn*, pl. *aʿyān*) are not the same. *Aʿyān thābita* is the term Ibn ʿArabī used to denote God's conceptual idea of species and objects He will make.[191] The word *taʿayyun* means individuation or manifestation in English. Once God executes the idea He had in mind – and creates minerals, for example – humans cannot change the manifested essence of minerals.[192] Gold and iron have the same essence, however, since they belong to the same species. Only their form (*ṣūra*) differs, because of the cosmological and metrological factors described in Section 5.

Like most of his contemporaries, Ibn ʿArabī used the word *ṣūra* as a synonym for the outward appearance of living beings, forms and objects. The related verbal noun, *taṣwīr*, denotes the shapeshifting abilities of human sorcerers, angels and jinn in his works.[193] Forms, unlike essences, are susceptible to change. 'Stones were never meant to assume multiple forms,' Ibn ʿArabī explained. 'God created them with a single perfect form in mind: gold.'[194] It is thus possible to turn iron into gold permanently. Alchemists merely seek to return mineral substances (*jawāhir*) to their original form.[195] We previously demonstrated that mineral substances are a form of gross matter, which consists of fire, water, air and earth. On his side, Ibn ʿArabī believed that all mineral substances stem from a single root (*aṣl*) and essence, whose nature is to seek the perfection of gold.[196] This root he identified as the divine name al-ʿAzīz.

190 FM.II: 621. FM.II: 372.

191 Chittick, *The Sufi Path of Knowledge*, p. 83.

192 FM.I: 236.

193 For instance, see Ibn ʿArabī, *K. Inshā' al-dawā'ir*, p. 2020. Here it should be noted that Ibn ʿArabī sometimes used the word *ṣūra* in a broader sense, to denote the human body (*jism*), soul (*nafs*) and spirit (*rūḥ*) combined. This is especially the case when he refers to the Qur'anic verses indicating that God made Adam in His form (Q. 95:4). Hence, the Akbarian concept of form should not be absolutely identified with the anatomy of humans. Mineral forms are simpler in comparison: they merely reflect the general health of mineral bodies and spirits (see Section 5 and FM.II: 235–236, FM.IV: 279 in particular).

194 FM.II 460.

195 Ibn ʿArabī, K. *Shaqq al-jayb*, p. 324.

196 FM.II: 271.

The prophet Muhammad spoke of the ninety-nine beautiful names of God repeatedly (*asmāʾ allāh al-ḥusnā*). There are sayings attributed to the prophet, which Ibn ʿArabī cited, that God wished to be known by humans. And so He made the world reflect the properties of His names.[197] Most living beings, forms and objects reflect the properties of one name only. Such is the case with the name al-ʿAzīz and minerals, for instance. This name means 'victorious' in Arabic, and it conveys the idea of strength, control and power. Minerals substances exhibit these properties – reflecting God's might (*ʿizza*) – which makes it hard for alchemists to bend them to their will. The divine name al-ʿAzīz also stands in the way of natural transmutations, causing them to last for millennia.[198] It does not make it ontologically impossible to turn iron into gold, however.

Ibn ʿArabī believed a successful alchemical transmutation means perfecting the outward form (*ṣūra*) and substance (*jawhar*) of iron, by ridding it of elemental disbalances.[199] Once the four elements a mineral substance consists of are brought into equilibrium, its outward form will change and turn to gold. There is not one way to achieve this goal. An alchemist could thus be compared to a good teacher, who will tailor their curriculum carefully so as to bring each of their students to God. No competent teacher will rely on the same method when instructing a student who is sharp and prone to analytical thinking (*naẓar*), and the one who is obedient but dull. Instead, they will provide hints and riddles for bright students and give strict orders to a duller person. Some alchemists Ibn ʿArabī encountered believed that metals deserve to be treated as individuals, like humans. And so they concocted elixirs suited to treat specific ailments (*ʿilla*) of a specific mineral. A mineral substance where water is the predominant element could be brought into equilibrium by exposure to sustained heat, for instance.[200] Ibn ʿArabī did not approve of this approach, however – nor did he concern himself with measures, weights and masses. The fact that Arab alchemists referred to their art as the Science of the Scale (*ʿilm al-mizān*) was of no importance to him since he felt that humans are prone to error when trying to measure things precisely.[201] Ibn ʿArabī advised prospective alchemists to do away with scales and seek red sulphur instead.

[197] FM.II: 167, 399.
[198] FM.II: 482–483.
[199] FM.I: 236. Comparable views can also be found in al-Irāqī, *Book of Knowledge*, p. 14. See also Wiedemann, 'Zur Alchemie bei den Arabern', pp. 115–123.
[200] FM.I: 153, 592–593; FM.II: 272–273.
[201] FM.II: 282.

7 The Alchemy of Red Sulphur

Alchemists of the West regarded sulphur with suspicions. They linked it with the Sun – with Jung claiming that the redness (*rubedo*) of sunlight signifies red sulphur – as well as flames, destruction, devils and dragons besides.[202] Arab alchemists differentiated between several types of sulphur: yellow and white, multi-coloured, black and red, with the red variant being the most prized of all.[203] Manfred Ullmann discovered alchemy manuals crediting the discovery of red sulphur to Cleopatra. The queen, who did know Arabic, was quoted saying that 'red sulphur' stands for all that is precious and rare.[204] This is a valid observation, irrespective of authorship. The term 'red sulphur' appears in Arabic literature as a synonym for phoenix eggs,[205] rain in the desert,[206] real friends,[207] intelligence,[208] human lives and the companions of the Prophet,[209] polite, respectful speech,[210] knowledge of God,[211] and ijtihad.[212] Ibn ʿArabī described it as one of God's treasures, which ought to be stored in the most fortified vaults for safekeeping.[213]

Al-Bīrūnī, who claimed to have seen red sulphur, found it sticky, soft and moist to the touch. The mineral al-Bīrūnī had in his possession was about the size of a fist. He did not hesitate to break it, which made him realize that red sulphur is translucent, rather than opaque. Al-Bīrūnī also took note of the reports claiming that red sulphur was bioluminescent. For instance, the story goes that when King Solomon saw that the building of Bayt al-Maqdis was at an end, he adorned the dome of the newly built temple with red sulphur, whose light could be seen from seven or twelve miles away.[214] Al-Bīrūnī's stone did not glow in the dark, however.

202 Jung, *Mysterim Coniunctions*, pp. 119–120, 126. See also Schwartz-Salant (ed.), *Jung on Alchemy*, p. 159, 162–163.
203 See al-Qazwīnī, *ʿAjāʾib al-makhlūqāt*, p. 213 and al-ʿUmarī, *Masālik al-abṣār fī mamālik al-amṣār*, vol. 22, p. 61, 360.
204 Ulmann, 'Kleopatra', p. 168.
205 al-Jawharī, *Al-Ṣiḥāḥ fī al-lugha wal-ʿulūm*, p. 4360.
206 Al-Hindī, *Kanz al-ummāl*, vol. 1, p. 624.
207 Badr al-Dīn, *ādāb al-ʿishra wa dhikr al-ṣuḥba wal-ukhuwwa*, p. 30.
208 Al-Albānī, *Ḍaʿīf al-jāmiʿ al-ṣaghīr*, p. 31.
209 al-Makkī, *Qūt al-Qulūb*, vol. 1, p. 93.
210 Al-Raḥīlī, *al-Akhlāq al-fāḍila*, p. 33.
211 Al-Ghazālį, *Jawāhir al-Qurʾān*, pp. 25–26, 56.
212 Al-Subkī, *Rafuʿ al-ḥājib mukhtaṣar Ibn al-Ḥājib*, vol. 4, p. 595.
213 Ibn ʿArabī, *K. al-Tadbīrāt al-ilāhiyya*, pp. 390–393.
214 For instance, see al-ʿAynī, *al-Bināya*, vol. 2, p. 471. A similar report can be found in al-ʿUmarī, *Masālik al-abṣār fī mamālik al-amṣār*, vol. 22, p. 61. To their credit, the quoted authors both claimed that bioluminescence would cease if red sulphur were to be removed from its native soil.

Worse still, it had no visible effect on silver. Not only did it fail to turn the lesser metal into gold, but it also deteriorated when brought in contact with heated silver. When al-Bīrūnī threw whatever he had left of it into the fire, the mineral ignited, and the distinct stench of sulphur filled the room. The fire burned deep crimson, mirroring the hue of the mineral itself. Al-Bīrūnī remarked upon its resemblance to rubies, and he surmised this likeness was what led scholars to believe that red sulphur was a type of ruby.[215] Sufi scholar Aḥmad al-Ghazālī (d. 1123) who was among proponents of this theory, differentiated between three types of red sulphur: red ruby (*al-yāqūt al-aḥmar*), brownish ruby (*al-yāqūt al-akhab*) and yellow ruby (*al-yāqūt al-aṣfar*).[216] 'Red ruby' and 'red sulphur' were also used interchangeably, as synonyms, for the heart of the Perfect Human in Ibn ʿArabī's works. The third chapter of *al-Futūḥāt* contains the following description of the perfect heart:

> The whole heart is like a polished mirror, with no rust on it. ... It is open for the arrival of divine unveilings, shining and pure. Every such heart, where the divine presence can manifest itself as it is, is a red ruby (*yāqut aḥmar*) – an essential unveiling in itself! Such is the heart of a witness [of divine unveilings and revelations], perfected and unsurpassable in knowledge.[217]

Ibn ʿArabī's students saw in this an apt description of the heart of their shaykh and, before long, they began referring to him as 'the Red Sulphur'.[218] The shaykh himself thought that every living being was profoundly influenced by their surroundings. Just as water takes the colour of its vessel, sorcerers consorting with fire spirits are bound to become as arrogant as the jinn-folk in time. Human greed can also corrupt precious stones and metals in our possession.[219] The heart of the Perfect Human has a positive impact on its surroundings in contrast, with Ibn ʿArabī's followers claiming to have (in)directly profited from it. 'Ibn ʿArabī was the very personification of alchemy', Ibrahīm b. ʿAbd Allāh Qārī (d. 1382) said,

> for the heart of alchemy, according to the masters of the craft, resides in transmuting essences, such that, through the action of the elixir, lead

215 al-Bīrūnī, *al-Jamāhir fī maʿarifa al-jawāhir*, p. 46.

216 The three types of red sulphur were used as symbols of the knowledge of 1) God's essence, 2) His attributes and 3) His deeds and actions in al-Ghazālī's works. al-Ghazālį, *Jawāhir al-Qurʾān*, pp. 25–26, 56.

217 FM.I: 91.

218 Stephen Hirtenstein dated the earliest reference to this title in Akbarian circles to 1250, ten years after Ibn ʿArabī's death. Hirtenstein, 'Names and Titles of Ibn [al-] ʿArabī', pp. 113–114.

219 FM.I: 559.

> turns into silver and copper into gold; thus, he – may God be pleased with him – was the elixir of his time and the alchemy of his age, for through his guidance how many of the essences [of his disciples] were turned from the common baseness of the animal soul into the preciousness of the true human being.[220]

The heart of the Perfect Human was believed to have the same power as the staff of Hermes and/or Midas's hand, which turned everything they touched into gold.[221] My Element will dwell no further on this metaphor, partly because the heart of the Perfect Human and its properties have been addressed in prior scholarship time and again.

Here it should be noted that Ibn ʿArabī believed humans were made to represent the perfect copy of the universe in miniature.[222] My Element is chiefly concerned red sulphur, the mineral, however, which is a macrocosmic counterpart of the heart of the Perfect Human. At times, Ibn ʿArabī referred to this mineral as the honourable stone (*al-ḥijr al-mukarram*), the philosophers' stone (*ḥijr al-falāsifa* or *ḥijr al-ḥukamāʾ*) and the elixir of felicity. Alternative names for red sulphur in alchemy manuals include the red bride (*al-ʿarūṣ al-ḥamrāʾ*), the bird of Socrates (*ṭayr Suqrāṭ*), the lion of earth (*asad al-arḍ*) and the ferment of gold (*khamīr al-dhahab*).[223] Not a few scholars believed red sulphur was identical to gold.[224] Ibn ʿArabī, however, argued that the former was impervious to change and corruption (which is not the case with gold).[225] Whatever red sulphur touches, it changes for the better; with Ibn ʿArabī claiming that God's intention when He made this mineral was to present humans with a proof that anyone could change. Were an infidel to get hold of red sulphur, they would turn to God and repent of their sins at once. Exposure to red sulphur causes enemies to let go of hatred and reconcile; it restores health and turns lesser stones and metals into gold.[226] Shams al-Dīn Ibn al-Jawzī (d. 1256) did

---

220 Quoted according to Todd, *The Sufi Doctrine of Man*, p. 63. Cf. Qārī, *Manāqib Ibn ʿArabī*, p. 41.

221 There are also records of alchemists using human hair and blood to refine common stones and metals. Marlow Taylor (trans.), *The Alchemy of al-Razi*, p. 263, 275. Further information on the staff of Hermes can be found at Lindsay, *The Origins of Alchemy in Graeco-Roman Egypt*, p. 33.

222 For instance, see Chittick (trans.), 'Ibn ʿArabī's own Summary of the Fuṣūṣ', pp. 10–11.

223 Twenty-two other synonyms for sulphur in Arabic, which were identified by Gabriele Fereirro, can be consulted at Fereirro, 'An Arabic Dictionary', p. 45.

224 For instance, see Dozi, *Takmila al-Maʿājim al-ʿarabiya*, vol. 9, p. 24; Aḥmad Riḍā, *Muʿajam matn al-lugha*, vol. 5, p. 12; Ibn al-Nadīm, *The Fihrist*, vol. 2, p. 921; al-Jawharī, *Al-Ṣiḥāḥ fī al-lugha wal-ulūm*, pp. 43–60; Al-Thaʿālabī, *al-Laṭāʾif wal-zarāʾif*, p. 197.

225 Ibn ʿArabī, *K. al-Tadbīrāt al-ilāhiyya*, pp. 390–393.

226 FM.II: 270-1, 282. See also Ibn ʿArabī, *K. al-Tadbīrāt al-ilāhiyya*, pp. 390–393. On the authority of Avicenna, common sulphur was also used in medicine to treat skin

not think it necessary for humans to possess red sulphur: just dreaming of it would be enough to endow a person with precious knowledge and insights.[227] But Ibn ʿArabī wished for more.

He noted a person would be wise to find themselves a guide to open the door of knowledge for them – if just a bit – when first embarking on the quest for red sulphur. If no competent guide can be found, a person ought to seclude themselves from the world to prepare for the journey. They should spend forty days away from other humans, thinking of God alone and chanting the following verse from the Qur'an: 'There is nothing like Him.'[228] Only then can the quest for red sulphur begin in earnest. Some authors recommended searching in the far west, on seashores, in darkness.[229] Deposits of red sulphur were reportedly found in Ibn ʿArabī's home country, Andalusia, as well as in China and the Maghreb.[230] Sources placed the biggest of deposits in the Valley of Ants, which is also mentioned in the Qur'an.[231] The book *K. Shaqq al-jayb*, which is traditionally attributed to Ibn ʿArabī, offers further hints on good places to look for red sulphur. Here, the reader is advised to journey in the direction of the equator, until they see a mountain reaching up to the heavens. On the top of that mountain a reservoir can be found, and a great dome besides. The reservoir contains deposits of sulphur, which ignites regularly under the light of the Sun, and is greatly prized among alchemists for its magical properties.[232] Although the text of *K. Shaqq al-jayb* does not contain the name of the mountain, its author in all likelihood had Mt Damavand in mind.

I believe this to be the case since al-Bīrūnī noted that the common folk insisted there was a spring and reservoir hidden at the top of Mt Damavand, filled with sulphur, which was the source of smoke rising from

---

blemishes, epilepsy, strokes, migraines and leprosy. See al-ʿUmarī, *Masālik al-abṣār fī mamālik al-amṣār*, vol. 22, p. 363.

227 Ibn al-Jawzī, *Mirʾāt al-zamān fī tārīkh al-ʿayān*, vol. 16, p. 457.

228 Ibn ʿArabī, *K. al-Tadbīrāt al-ilāhiyya*, pp. 390–393. The verses in question are from the surah al-Shūrā, which describes God as 'the Creator of heavens and earth. He made for you spouses from among yourselves, like he made mates for cattle to multiply. There is nothing like Him, the All-Hearing, the All-Seeing' (Q. 42:11).

229 al-Makkī, *Qūt al-Qulūb*, vol. 1, p. 93; al-ʿUmarī, *Masālik al-abṣār fī mamālik al-amṣār*, vol. 22, p. 360.

230 See al-Bīrūnī, *al-Jamāhir fī maʿarifa al-jawāhir*, p. 46; Ibn al-Wardī, *Kharīda al-ʿajāʾib wa farīda al-gharāʾib.*, p. 277; al-Bakrī, *al-Masālik wal-mamālik*, vol. 2, p. 98 and al-Qazwīnī, *ʿAjāʾib al-makhlūqāt*, p. 213.

231 Yāqūt, Mu'ajam al-buldān, vol. 2, p. 11; al-Zabīdī, *Tāj al-arūs min jawāhir al-qāmūs*, p. 54; al-Zamakhsharī, *al-Mustaqṣā fī amthāl al-ʿarab*, vol. 1, p. 245. Cf. Q. 27:18.

232 Ibn ʿArabī, K. *Shaqq al-jayb*, p. 332.

the mountain.[233] There are numerous reports containing descriptions of Mt Damavand and red sulphur that match the information provided in *K. Shaqq al-jayb*, namely: that the mountain is so high it touches the sky and is perpetually covered in snow; and that near the top of the mountain a reservoir can be found containing deposits of sulphur which ignite under the Sun and cause the smoke to rise from the mountain. The reports invariably cite Masᶜūd b. Muhalhal of Khorasan, the alchemist, as their source of information. Masᶜūd noted that red sulphur is incredibly difficult to handle since it melts iron pots and tongs, and there are also snakes protecting the spring at Mt Damavand. Careful preparations and special mining techniques were required to excavate this mineral and have it delivered safely to the royal court in Khorasan.[234] Neither Masᶜūd nor Mt Damavand were mentioned in *K. Shaqq al-jayb* by name, however.

On his side, Osman Yahya questioned the authenticity of *K. Shaqq al-jayb*, since none of the thirteen surviving manuscripts of this work predates 1002 AH. Stephen Hirtenstein and Jane Clarke were later able to determine that the text comprises of a series of extracts from Ibn ᶜArabī's works, some of which are now lost.[235] Unfortunately, Ibn ᶜArabī's treatise which served as the original source of information on red sulphur and Mt Damavand from *K. Shaqq al-jayb* is among these lost works – with another possibility being that the information was appropriated from the writings of another scholar and falsely ascribed to Ibn ᶜArabī. Spiritual advice from *K. Shaqq al-jayb* thus ought to be taken with a grain of salt – not least because Ibn ᶜArabī's magnum opus *al-Futūḥāt*, whose authenticity is undisputed, advised spiritual practitioners to search for red sulphur in Mecca instead. There, owing to the favourable influence of the fourth clime, red sulphur and the perfect heart can be obtained simultaneously. Or so the poem goes:

> Tell me, friend, which place you want me to take you to.
> I want to go to the city of the Messenger, in search
> of the Station of Radiance and red sulphur![236]

---

233 al-Bīrūnī, *al-Jamāhir fī maᶜarifa al-jawāhir*, p. 46.

234 For instance, see Ibn al-Wardī, *Kharīdat al-ᶜajāʾib wa farīdat al-gharāʾib*, p. 280; al-Qazwīnī, *ʿAjāʾib al-makhlūqāt*, p. 151 and al-Qazwīnī, *āthāt al-bilād wa akhbār al-ʿibād*, p. 345.

235 'Mias Archive Report: the Catalogue of Ibn Arabī's Works,' Muhyiddin Ibn Arabi Society, accessed June 5, 2025, https://tinyurl.com/3psnkpar.

236 Quoted according to Addas, *Quest for the Red Sulphur*, vi. Cf. FM.I: 93.

8 In Conclusion

Prior sections of my Element delved into alchemical sources, traditions and the causes of corruption in the kingdom of minerals. The Element furthermore examined whether it is possible to turn lesser stones and metals into gold (it is, according to Ibn ʿArabī) and how this can be done (with the help of elixirs, red sulphur and *himma*). The Element concludes with words of caution: the fact that something *could* be done does not necessarily mean it *should.*

Ibn ʿArabī strongly believed that alchemical pursuits are feasible but ill advised. Not that he was opposed to wealth (*khayr*) in general. For although God promised hellfire to those who hoard gold and silver, Ibn ʿArabī knew that the word *khayr* could serve to indicate riches and goodness alike in Arabic. No true alchemist is hungry for riches, with Ibn ʿArabī maintaining that greed is a prerogative of frauds.[237] Alchemists rather seek to better the world of nature.

Christian alchemists such as Thomas Tymme (d. 1620), for example, aspired to do the same. They thought that the first sin and the Fall turned nature into a harsh and unforgiving place. Thus, they saw it as their duty to undo the harm the first humans caused.[238] Julian Baggini noted that humanity largely falls into two extremes: they either disregard the sentient nature of most species completely, treating them as commodities and resources, or think of 'animals as though they were a four-legged, feathered or finned version of ourselves, creatures who deserve a long life and for whom death at anything other than an old age is a tragedy'.[239] American wildlife conservationist William David Forman, for instance, sought to convince the world to do away with humanism, insisting that human life holds no greater value than that of a tree or bug.[240] Forman's uncompromising stance aligns with Ian Bogost's definition of posthumanism, which sought to elevate all living beings to the same status as humanity.[241] While his radical vision is not universally accepted among posthumanists, Cary Wolfe similarly denounced the way unequal relationships between nonhumans and humans are 'being taken for granted as an ethical (non)

[237] FM.I: 547.

[238] Tymme defined alchemy as 'a science whereby the principles, causes, properties and passions of all methals that are thoroughly knowne & discovered and by which those metals that are imperfect are corrupted, are altered and changed into true & perfect Gold'. Janacek, *Alchemical Belief*, p. 3, 17, 26. See also Smith, *The Business of Alchemy*, p. xv.

[239] Baggini, *How the World Eats*, p. 237.

[240] Forman, *Confessions of Eco Warrior*, pp. 3–4.

[241] Bogost, *Alien Phenomenology*, p. 7.

issue'.[242] Another posthumanist, Steve Beker, felt that human ethics was self-centred; it reflected a form of moral narcissism where concern for animal welfare mostly serves to ease our guilty consciences.[243] This is how euphemisms for murder appear in the everyday speech, according to Noëlie Vialles and Nicole Schukin. Vialles and Schukin paid close attention to the word 'abattoir' in particular, and how it pertains to the killing of animals in slaughterhouses. The original meaning of this word in French is 'to cause something to fall', and it was chiefly used in forestry and 'in the mineral world where it denoted the action of detaching mineral from the walls of a mine tunnel'.[244] Nowadays, however, 'abattoir' has become a euphemism obscuring the brutality of mass industrial slaughter. On his side, Cary Wolfe maintained there is no escaping the fact a horse is more intelligent than a human infant. Wolfe nonetheless thought the question of whether animals could reason and recall irrelevant. What matters is their indisputable capacity to suffer; this calls for human accountability.[245] In his works, Ibn ʿArabī also extended this capacity to suffer to plants and minerals.

Ibn ʿArabī did not share the belief of the early modern Christian alchemist that minerals and plants have no souls,[246] and he found them capable of complex emotions, religious worship and speech (see Section 3). Ibn ʿArabī's students were forbidden from felling trees and moving stones around unnecessarily, on the threat of damnation.[247] This is not to say, however, that Ibn ʿArabī valued the well-being of animals, plants and minerals over human comfort. There are limits to compassion in Akbarian Sufism.

242 Wolfe, *What Is Posthumanism?*, p. 49

243 Baker, *Artist|Animal*, p. 1, 64.

244 Quoted according to: Shukin, *Animal Capital*, p. 62. See also Vialles, *Animals to Edibles*, p. 22–23. Vialles and Schukin evidently had no problems with humans (ab)using minerals. Ibn ʿArabī did.

245 Wolfe, *What Is Posthumanism?*, pp. 33–34, 45. Wolfe based his argument on *Kinds of Minds* by Daniel Dennet.

246 Janacek, *Alchemical Belief*, p. 122. How mineral souls were perceived in Akbarian circles was discussed in Section 3.

247 People once believed a change in climate could cause the death of living beings, even if they were to be moved to countries under the influence of the fourth clime, which is the best of the seven climes. *Kitāb al-Masālik wa al-Mamālik*, which is a classical work on geography by Abū ʿAbd Allāh al-Bakrī (d. 1094), contains reports of Slavs dying once they were forcefully removed from their homeland, as the change of climate and warmth in particular did not suit their cold temperaments. al-Bakrī, *The Geography of al-Andalus and Europe*, pp. 182–183. Ibn ʿArabī thus forbade his students to relocate stones, so as not to harm them. See FM.I: 274, 710; FM.II: 460 and Ibn ʿArabī, *K. al-khalwa*, p. 157. Cf. Ibn ʿArabī, K. *Shaqq al-jayb*, p. 311.

Although Ibn ʿArabī did not condone senseless cruelty in forestry, farming and mining, this did not prevent him from mocking those who exalted earth and nature, which God made to be lowly (*jaʿala Allāh dhalūlan*). He did not share the views expressed in *Epistles of the Brethren of Purity*, which posited that bees and plants, water and soil, exist for their own sake. Rather, God had them made to serve and obey Muhammad (and other humans besides). 'Verily, I created the world for you, Muhammad, to serve as your kingdom!', Ibn ʿArabī heard Him say.[248] God also revealed to Ibn ʿArabī that celestial bodies and spheres above the Earth exist just so that humans could tell the time.[249] Ibn ʿArabī did not think that justice dictates for God to treat all species equally, nor did he think Him a sadist for creating the world of nature, red in tooth and claw. Wolves are not evil for devouring a deer, which God made to satiate their hunger. The Qur'an affirms He likewise provided humans with grains and cattle (Q. 16:5; 36:33), and He made iron 'useful and strong for the benefits of humankind' (Q. 57:26). God actively hinders the spiritual development of minerals, since it would be inconvenient for humans if all of them were to become gold.[250] An alchemist seeking to transmutate common stones and metals opposes His will directly. Hence, alchemy could be seen as an affront to God and a crime against humankind, whom alchemists seek to deprive of iron and copper, aluminium, zinc and steel.

An alchemist attempting to take away the gifts God bestowed on humankind may think themselves altruistic (assuming their efforts are rooted in general concern for the happiness and well-being of stones and metals). Ibn ʿArabī sought to convince his readers that their alchemical aspirations were misguided nonetheless. One of the arguments he made is that the world is already perfect as it is: God himself has seen to it. Tailor-made for humans, His perfect world allows for sickness and suffering in the kingdom of minerals, plants and animals.[251] Minerals, unlike humans, would never dream of perverting the world order He perfected, even if it

[248] FM.I: 4. See also FM.I 173. A similar sentiment was expressed in the Bible: 'Lord, you made humans rulers over the works of your hands; you put everything under their feet: all flocks and herds, and the animals of the wild, the birds in the sky, and the fish in the sea, all that swim the paths of the seas. Lord, our Lord, how majestic is your name in all the earth!' (Psalm 8). Cf. Goodman-McGregor (trans.), *The Case of the Animals versus Man before the King of the Jinn: A Translation from the Epistles of the Brethren of Purity*, p. 35.

[249] FM.I: 120.

[250] The divine name the Afflictor (ar. *al-Ḍārr*) plays a key role in this process. It corrupts minerals and turns them away from the path of perfection. FM.II: 420–421, 460–461.

[251] FM.I: 37.

means they will never become gold. The obedience of minerals to God is absolute, making them akin to angels.[252] Human do-gooders thus need to ask themselves whether they are prepared to subject minerals to alchemical transmutations against their will. This is the second argument that could be made against alchemy. Even if both these arguments were to be disregarded, Ibn ʿArabī forewarned prospective alchemists that no person could stand against God. Were humanity to present a unified front against Him, they would still fail to abolish the world order He established.[253] Ibn ʿArabī noted that God hinders most alchemical transmutations.[254] Only a small percentage are permitted to succeed.

Ibn ʿArabī's understanding was that the royal art is a prerogative of the worthy, whom God himself entrusted with the knowledge of alchemy: 'They are the ones He deemed worthy of preserving the wisdom He established in the world,' he explained.[255] In Section 4 we saw that Ibn ʿArabī counted himself among those who had a chance to learn from God. The alchemists He trained are no misguided altruists. They are reconciled with the fact He has afflicted countless stones and metals with sicknesses, and they allow the sickness and corruption of iron to persist

> because of the unique benefits [the afflicted] iron holds, which are not found in gold or other metals. God said He *brought down iron* in the Qur'an (Q. 57:25), and by this He meant that He brought it down from the station of perfection [which is gold], for the benefit of humankind. If iron were to be cured of illness, it would become too noble and its specific benefits would be lost, depriving humanity of tools and weapons.[256]

The duty of alchemists, the way Ibn ʿArabī saw it, was to keep the world in balance and preserve the natural order of things He established.

A sorcerer is slave to passions and the will to power, bending the laws of nature on a whim. A sage (*ʿārif*), by contrast, withholds their power unless God orders them to act.[257] This alignment with the divine command guarantees the success of their alchemical transmutations. A spell cast with selfish goals in mind is likely to fail, exposing the sorcerer to the ridicule of the world. Sometimes, however, God allows for the dark arts to thrive, with Ibn ʿArabī claiming he had encountered African

---

[252] FM.II: 10.
[253] FM.I: 37.
[254] FM.II: 460–461.
[255] FM.II: 461.
[256] In Europe, alchemy was also seen as a prerogative of a gentleman. Smith, *The Business of Alchemy*, p. 5. See also FM.II: 461.
[257] See FM.I: 112, 188; FM.II: 526–527 and Ibn Arabī, *ʿMawāqiʿ al-nujūm*, p. 58.

sorcerers who could kill other humans with *himma*.[258] A wicked sorcerer also severs as a regulating finger of God, whether they realize it or not. Ibn ʿArabī explained this applies to all humans to a degree. Namely, what most humans fail to realize is that God is the only active agent (*fāʿil*) in the universe. A person may believe they owe something to someone who helped them in need. But it is actually God who made the victim cry out for help, and He also made others answer their pleas. God is not deaf to the cries of minerals, Ibn ʿArabī maintained.[259] Sometimes, He answers the prayers of iron by allowing a sorcerer to turn it into gold. The sorcerer in question then thinks themselves mighty – although God was the one who initiated the transmutation process and saw it to completion. God made red sulphur for a reason – to serve as a proof that everything can change, Ibn ʿArabī explained, including common stones and metals – and He also made it rare, since it is not generally desirable for humans to try to change the world order He established.

When precious stones and metals are discussed in Islam, the discourse tends to revolve around *zakat* and the spiritual development of humans. Here, the goal was to move away from the anthropocentric point of view and Heidegger's object-oriented philosophy, which argues that 'objects' like bricks and hammers, for example, cannot be understood outside of whatever purpose humans have for them.[260] This is the predominating attitude towards minerals in Akbarian circles as well. My Element has sought to bring Ibn ʿArabī's understudied notions of alchemy to the forefront and make the voices of stones and metals heard.

Now, who would want to hear about the secret lives of minerals, their thoughts and fears? Anna Tsing asked herself the same when writing about *Bursaphelenchus xylophilus*, a small eelworm.[261] My Element took that risk, leaving it to the Greatest Shaykh – his name and fame – and the age-old hunger for gold to entice the reader to delve deeper into the kingdom of minerals.

[258] FM.I: 259; FM.II: 385, 526.
[259] FM.II: 263.
[260] Heidegger, *Being and Time*, p. 69, 343–345.
[261] Tsing, *The Mushroom at the End of the World*, p. 156.

Bibliography

Abdel-hadi, Faris. (2025). *Ibn ʿArabī's Religious Pluralism: Levels of Inclusivity*. London: Routledge.

Abraham, Lyndyn. (1998). *A Dictionary of Alchemical Imagery*. Cambridge: Cambridge University Press.

Addas, Claude. (1993). *Quest for the Red Sulphur: The Life of Ibn ʿArabī*. Cambridge: The Islamic Text Society.

Aḥmad Riḍā. (1958). *Muʿajam matn al-lugha*, vol. 5. Beirut: Dār maktaba al-ḥayāt.

al-Albānī, Naṣr al-Dīn. (2013). *Ḍaʿīf al-jāmiʿ al-ṣaghīr*. Damascus: al-Maktaba al-Islāmī.

Alegre, Juan Udaono. (2024). *The Spanish Hermes and Wisdom Traditions in Medieval Iberia*. Durham: Durham University Press.

Anawati, Georges. (1996). 'Arabic Alchemy'. In Roshdi Rashed, ed., *Encyclopedia of the History of Arabic Science*, vol. 3. London: Routledge, pp. 853–886.

Aristotle. (1951). *Meteorologica*, translated by H. D. P. Lee. Cambridge, MA: Harvard University Press.

Averroes, Abū al-Walīd Muḥammad. (1962). *Aristotelis opera cum Averrois commentariis*, vol. 6. Frankfurt: Minerva.

Avicenna, Abū ʿAlī al-Ḥusayn (1927). *De congelatione et conglutinatione lapidum, Being Sections of Kitāb al-Shifāʾ*. The Latin and Arabic Text, edited and translated by E. J. Holmyard and D. C. Mandeville. Paris: Paul Geuthner.

al-ʿAynī, Badr al-Dīn. (2002). *al-Bināya*, vol. 2. Beirut: Dār al-kutub al-ʿilmiya.

Al-Azmeh, Aziz. (1992). 'Barbarians in the Arab Eyes'. *Past & Present*, 134, 3–18.

Bacon, Roger. (1597). *The Mirror of Alchemy*. London: Printed for Richard Oliue.

Badr al-Dīn, Muḥammad. (1968). *ādāb al-ʿishra wa dhikr al-ṣuḥba wal-ukhuwwa*. Damascus: Maṭbūʿāt majmaʿ al-lugha al-ʿarabiyya.

Baggini, Julian. (2024). *How the World Eats: A Global Food Philosophy*. London: Granta Publications.

Baker, Steve. (2013). *Artist|Animal*. Minneapolis: University of Minnesota Press.

al-Bakrī, Abū ʿUbayd. (1968). *The Geography of al-Andalus and Europe: From the Book Al-masālik wal-mamālik*. Beirut: Dār al-irshād.

al-Bakrī, Abū ʿUbayd. (1992). *Al-masālik wal-mamālik*, vol. 2. Tunisia: Dār al-gharb al-islāmī.

Beretta, Marco. (2009). *Alchemy of Glass: Counterfeit, Imitation, and Transmutation in Ancient Glassmaking*. Cambridge: Science History Pubns.

al-Bīrūnī, Abū al-Rayḥān. (n.d.). *Al-Jamāhir fī maʿarifa al-jawāhir*. Cairo: Maktaba Shāmela.

al-Bīrūnī, Abū al-Rayḥān. K. Taḥdid al-amākin. (1967). *The Determination of the Coordinates of Positions for the Correction of Distances between Cities*, translated by Jamil Ali. Beirut: The American University of Beirut.

Bogost, Ian. (2012). *Alien Phenomenology, or What It's Like to Be a Thing*. Minneapolis: University of Minnesota Press.

Bosnevi, Abdullah. (2003). *Marātib al-wujūd. Gradacija Bitka*, translated by Kenan Čemo and Samir Beglerović. Sarajevo: Libris.

Bosnevi, Abdullah. (2009). *Sharḥ Fuṣūṣ al-ḥikam*, translated by Rašid Hafizović. Sarajevo: Institute Ibn Sina.

Braun, Christoper. (2016). '"Who Began This Art? From Whence Did It Emerge?": A Hermetic Frame Story on the Origins of Alchemy in Pseudo-Ibn Waḥshīya's The Book of the Ziziphus. Tree of the Furthest Boundary'. *Al-Qantara*, 37, 373–398.

Brethren of Purity. (2011). *On Magic, Part I: An Arabic Critical Edition and English Translation of Epistle 52a*, edited and translated by Godefroid de Callataÿ and Bruno Halflants. Oxford: Oxford University Press.

Brethren of Purity. (2014). *On the Natural Sciences: An Arabic Critical Edition and English Translation of Epistles 15–21*, edited and translated by Carmela Baffioni. Oxford: Oxford University Press.

Bull, Christian. (2018). *The Tradition of Hermes Trismegustus: The Egyptian Priestly Figure as a Teacher of Hellenized Wisdom*. Leiden: Brill.

Bull, Christian. (2018). 'Wicked Angels and the Good Demon'. *Gnosis: Journal of Gnostic Studies*, 3, 3–33.

Burckhardt, Titus. (1972). *Alchemy: Science of the Cosmos, Science of the Soul*. New York: Penguin.

Burnett, Charles. (1992). 'The Astrologer's Assay of the Alchemist'. *Ambix*, 39, 104–109.

Burrus, Virginia. 1995. *The Making of a Heretic: Gender, Authority, and the Priscillianist Controversy*. Oakland: University of California Press.

Chassinat, Emile. (1931). *Le temple d'Edfou*, vol. 6. Cairo: IFAO.

Chittick, William (trans.). (1982). 'Ibn ʿArabī's Own Summary of the Fuṣūṣ'. *Journal of the Muhyiddin Ibn Arabi Society*, 1, 88–128.

Chittick, William. (1989). *The Sufi Path of Knowledge: Ibn ʿArabī's Metaphysics of Imagination*. Albany: State University of New York Press.

Dajani, Samer. (2024). *Sufis and Sharīʿa. The Forgotten School of Mercy*. Edinburgh: Edinburgh University Press.

Debus, Allen. (2006). *The Chemical Promise: Experiment and Mysticism in the Chemical Philosophy, 1550–1800*. Cambridge: Science History Pubns.

Dennett, Daniel. (1996). *Kinds of Minds: Toward an Understanding of Consciousness*. New York: Basic Books.

Dozi, Reinhart. (2000). *Takmila al-Maʿājim al-ʿarabiya*, vol. 9. Baghdad: Wazāra al-thaqāfa.

Dubs, Homer. (1947). 'The Beginnings of Alchemy'. *Isis*, 38, 62–86.

Dym, Warren Alexander. (2008). 'Alchemy and Mining: Metallogenesis and Prospecting in Early Mining Books'. *Ambix*, 55, 232–254.

Elmore, Gerald. (1995). 'Fabulous Gryphon (ʿAnqāʾ Mughrib) on the Seal of the Saints and the Sun Rising in the West', PhD diss., Yale University.

Emerton, Norma. (1984). *The Scientific Reinterpretation of Form*. Ithaca: Cornell University Press.

Fereirro, Gabrielle. (2009). 'An Arabic Dictionary of Technical Alchemical Terms: MS Sprenger 1908 of the Staatsbibliothek zu Berlin (fols. 3r–6r)'. *Ambix*, 56, 36–48.

Flequer, Jaime. (2023). 'The Science of Letters and Alchemy in Ibn ʿArabī's Jesus'. *Religions* 14, 1–14.

Fodor, A. (1970). 'The Origins of Arabic Legends'. *Acta Orientalia Academiae Scientiarum Hungaricae*, 23, 335–363.

Forman, William David. (1991). *Confessions of Eco Warrior*. New York: Crown Publishers Inc.

Forster, Regula. (2016). 'Arabic Alchemy: Texts and Contexts'. *Al-Qantara*, 37, 269–278.

Forster, Regula. (2019). 'Zwischen Religion und Alchemie: Der Gelehrte Ibn Arfaʿ Raʾs (fl. 12. Jh.)'. *SGMOIK SSMOCI Bulletin*, 48, 11–15.

Frankopan, Peter. (2023). *The Earth Transformed: An Untold History*. New York: Knopf Publishing Group.

Gauthier, Henri and Sottas Henri. (1925). *Un décret trilingue en l'honneur de Ptolémée IV*. Cairo: IFAO.

al-Ghazālī, Abū Ḥāmid. (1986). *Jawāhir al-Qur'ān*. Beirut: Dār iḥyā' al-'ulūm.

Goodman, Leen E. and McGregor, Richard (trans.). (2012). *The Case of the Animals versus Man before the King of the Jinn: A Translation from the Epistles of the Brethren of Purity*. Oxford: Oxford University Press.

Gosden, Chris. (2021). *The History of Magic: From Alchemy to Witchcraft, from the Ice Age to the Present*. London: Penguin.

Graefe, Erich (trans.). (1911). *Das Pyramidenkapitel in Al-Makrīzī's 'Ḫiṭaṭ'*. Leipzig: J. C. Hinrichs.

Grafton, Anthony. (2023). *Magus: The Art of Magic from Faustus to Agrippa*. London: Penguin Books.

Gutas, Dimitri. (1998). *Greek Thought, Arabic Culture: The Graeco-Arabic Translation Movement in Baghdad and Early 'Abbāsid Society*. London: Routledge.

Hamarneh, Sami. (1982). 'Arabic-Islamic Alchemy – The Three Intertwined Stages'. *Ambix*, 29, 74–87.

Hanegraaf, Wouter. (2013). *Western Esotericism: A Guide for the Perplexed*. London: Bloomsbury Academic.

Haq, Syed Nomannul. (1994). *Names, Natures and Things: The Alchemist Jābir ibn Ḥayyān and his Kitāb al-Aḥjār (Book of Stones)*. Dordrecht: Kluwer Academic Publishing.

Harvey, Steven. (1992). 'A New Islamic Source of the *Guide of the Perplexed*'. In Arthur Hyman, ed., *Maimonidean Studies*, vol. 2. New York: Yeshiva University Press, pp. 31–59.

Hassan, Ahmad. (2009). *Studies in al-Kimiya'. Critical Issues in Latin and Arabic Alchemy and Chemistry*. New York: Georg Olms Verlag.

Heidegger, Martin. (2010). *Being and Time*, translated by Joan Stambaugh. Albany: State University of New York Press.

al-Hindī, 'Alā al-Dīn al-Muttaqī. (1958). *Kanz al-ummāl fī sunan al-aqwāl wal-af'āl*, vol. 1. Damascus: Mu'asas al-risāla.

Hirtenstein, Stephen (trans.). (2017). *The Alchemy of Human Happiness (fi marifat kimiyà' al-sa ada)*. Oxford: Anqa Publishing.

Hirtenstein, Stephen (ed.). (1993). *Muhyiddin Ibn Arabi: A Commemorative Volume*. Oxford: Muhyiddin Ibn Arabi Society.

Hirtenstein, Stephen. (2007). 'Names and Titles of Ibn [al-]'Arabī'. *Journal of Muhyiddin Ibn Arabi Society*, 41, 109–131.

Hirtenstein, Stephen. (1999). *The Unlimited Mercifier: The Spiritual Life and Thought of Ibn 'Arabī*. Oxford: Anqa Publishing.

Holland, Tom. (2023). *Pax: War and Peace in Rome's Golden Age*. London: Abacus.

Holmyard, E. J. (1957). *Alchemy*. London: Penguin.

Holmyard, E. J. and Russel, Richard (eds.). (2010). *The Works of Geber*. Whitefish: Kessinger Publishing.

Hopkins, Arthur John. (1934). *Alchemy, Child of Greek Philosophy*. New York: Columbia University Press.

Hughes, Jonathan. (2012). *The Rise of Alchemy in Fourteenth-Century England. Plantagenet Kings and the Search for the Philosopher's Stone*. New York: Continuum International Publishing Group.

Ibn ʿArabī, Muhyī al-Dīn Abū ʿAbd Allāh. (1980). *The Bezels of Wisdom*, translated by Ralph W. J. Austin. New York: Paulist Press.

Ibn ʿArabī, Muhyī al-Dīn Abū ʿAbd Allāh. (1997). 'Divine Governance of the Human Kingdom'. In Tosun Bayrak al-Jerrahi al-Halveti, ed., *Al-Tadbīrāt al-Ilāhiya fī Iṣlāḥ al-Mamlaka al-Insāniya*. Louisville: Fons Vitae.

Ibn ʿArabī, Muhyī al-Dīn Abū ʿAbd Allāh. (1859). *Al-Futūḥāt al-Makkiyya*, 4 vols. Cairo: n.d.

Ibn ʿArabī, Muhyī al-Dīn Abū ʿAbd Allāh. (617 AH). *Kitāb al-Mīm (MS Veliyuddin 1759)*. Konya: Bayezit Devlet Kütüphanesi.

Ibn ʿArabī, Muhyī al-Dīn Abū ʿAbd Allāh. (2004). *Kitāb ʿAnqāʾ mughrib: Rasāʾil Ibn ʿArabī 4*. Beirut: Arab Diffusion Company.

Ibn ʿArabī, Muḥyī al-Dīn Abū ʿAbd Allāh. (1919). 'Inshāʾ al-dawāʾir wa al-jadāwil'. In H. S. Nyberg, ed., *Kleinere Schriften des Ibn ʿArabī*. Leiden: Brill, pp. 1–60.

Ibn ʿArabī, Muhyī al-Dīn Abū ʿAbd Allāh. (2015). *Kitāb al-Isfār ʿan natāʾij al-asfār. The Secrets of Voyaging*, edited and translated by Angela Jaffray. Oxford: Anqa Publishing.

Ibn ʿArabī, Muhyī al-Dīn Abū ʿAbd Allāh. (2006). *Kitāb al-khalwa. Rasāʾil Ibn ʿArabī 6*. Beirut: Arab Diffusion Company.

Ibn ʿArabī, Muhyī al-Dīn Abū ʿAbd Allāh. (2001). *Kitāb Manzil al-manāzil. Rasāʾil Ibn ʿArabī 1*. Beirut: Arab Diffusion Company.

Ibn ʿArabī, Muhyī al-Dīn Abū ʿAbd Allāh. (2004). *Kitab al-maʿarif. Rasāʾil Ibn ʿArabī 4*. Beirut: Arab Diffusion Company.

Ibn ʿArabī, Muhyī al-Dīn Abū ʿAbd Allāh. (2001). *Kitāb Shaqq al-jayb. Rasāʾil Ibn ʿArabī 1*. Beirut: Arab Diffusion Company.

Ibn ʿArabī, Muhyī al-Dīn Abū ʿAbd Allāh. (2002). *Kitāb al-Tadbīrāt al-ilāhiyya fī Iṣlāḥ al-Mamlaka al-Insāniya. Rasāʾil Ibn ʿArabī 2*. Beirut: Arab Diffusion Company.

Ibn ʿArabī, Muhyī al-Dīn Abū ʿAbd Allāh. (2005). *Kitāb al-Qasam al-ilāhī. Rasāʾil Ibn ʿArabī 5*. Beirut: Arab Diffusion Company.

Ibn ʿArabī, Muhyī al-Dīn Abū ʿAbd Allāh. (2001). *Kitāb al-Quṭb wal-imāmayn. Rasāʾil Ibn ʿArabī 1*. Beirut: Arab Diffusion Company.

Ibn ʿArabī, Muhyī al-Dīn Abū ʿAbd Allāh. (2004). *Kitāb al-yaqīn. Rasāʾil Ibn ʿArabī 4*. Beirut: Arab Diffusion Company.

Ibn ʿArabī, ʾAbū ʿAbd Allāh Muḥammad. (2007). *Mawāqiʿ al-nujūm wa-maṭāliʿ ʾahillat al-ʾasrār wa-al-ʿulūm*. Beirut: Dār al-kutub al-ʾilmiyya.

Ibn ʿArabī, Muhyī al-Dīn Abū ʿAbd Allāh. (2002). *Risāla al-anwār. Rasāʾil Ibn ʿArabī 2*. Beirut: Arab Diffusion Company.

Ibn ʿArabī, Muhyī al-Dīn Abū ʿAbd Allāh. (2006). *Sḥarh tarjumān al-ashwāq. Rasāʾil Ibn ʿArabī 5*. Beirut: Arab Diffusion Company.

Ibn ʿArabī, Muhyī al-Dīn Abū ʿAbd Allāh. (2008). *Sufis of Andalusia: From the Rūh al-Quds and al-Durrat al-Fākirah*, translated by R. W. J. Austin. London: Routledge.

Ibn ʿArabī, Muhyī al-Dīn Abū ʿAbd Allāh. (2002). *ʿUqlat al-mustawfiz. Rasāʾil Ibn ʿArabī 2*. Beirut: Arab Diffusion Company.

Ibn al-Jawzī, Shams al-Dīn. (2013). *Mirʾāt al-zamān fī tārīkh al-ʿayān*, vol. 16. Beirut: Dār al-risāla al-ʿālamiyya.

Ibn Jubayr, Abū al-Ḥusayn. (1952). *The Travels of Ibn Jubayr: A Medieval Journey from Cordoba to Jerusalem*, translated by R. J. C. Broadhurst. London: Jonathan Cape.

Ibn Khaldūn, Abū Zayd ʿAbd al-Raḥmān. (1980). *al-Muqaddima*, vol. 3. New Jersey: Princeton University Press.

Ibn al-Nadīm, Muḥammad b. Isḥāq. (1970). *The Fihrist: A Tenth-Century Survey of Muslim Culture*, vol. 2, translated by Bayard Dodge. New York: Columbia University Press.

Ibn Umayl, Muḥammad. (2020). *Durra an-naqlya*. The Precious Pearl, edited and translated by Theodor Abt. Zurich: Living Human Heritage Publications.

Ibn Waḥshiyya, Aḥmad. (1806). *Ancient Alphabets and Hieroglyphic Characters Explained*, translated by Joseph Hammer. London: W. Bulmer and Co.

Ibn al-Wardī, Sirāj al-Dīn. (2008). *Kharīda al-ʿajāʿib wa farīda al-gharāʿib*. Cairo: Maktaba al-thaqāfa al-islāmiyya.

al-Irāqī, Abū al-Qāsim Muḥammad. (2018). *Book of Knowledge Acquired Concerning the Cultivation of Gold*, edited and translated by E. J. Holmyard. Eastford: Martino Fine Books.

Janacek, Bruce. (2011). *Alchemical Belief: Occultism in the Religious Culture of Early Modern England.* University Park: Penn State University Press.

al-Jawharī, Abū Naṣr. (1974). *Al-Ṣiḥāḥ fī al-lugha wal-ulūm.* Beirut: Dār al-ḥaḍāra al-ʿarabiya.

John of Damascus. (1958). *Writings*, translated by Frederic H. Chase. Washington, DC: The Catholic University of America Press.

Jung, Carl Gustav. (1977). *Mysterim Coniunctions*, translated by R. F. C. Hull. New Jersey: Princeton University Press.

Kambylus, A. (ed.). (2008). *Ioannis Antiocheni fragment aquae supersunt omnia.* Berlin: De Gruyter.

Karpenko, Vladímir. (2003). 'Systems of Metals in Alchemy'. *Ambix*, 50, 208–230.

Kramer, Heinrich. (2007). *Malleus maleficarum*, edited and translated by P. G. Maxwell-Stuart. New York: Manchester University Press.

Kraus, Paul. (1994). *Alchemie, Ketzerei, Apokryphen in frühen Islam.* Hildesheim: Georg Olms Verlag.

Lala, Ismail. (2023). 'Turning Religious Experience into Reality'. *Religions*, 14, 1–16.

Landau, Rom. (1959). *The Philosophy of Ibn Arabi.* London: Routledge.

Levey, Martin. (1967). 'Arabic Mineralogy of the Tenth Century'. *Chymia*, 12, 15–26.

Linden, J. Stanton. (2003). *The Alchemy Reader: From Hermes Trismegistus to Isaac Newton.* Cambridge: Cambridge University Press.

Lindsay, Jack. (1970). *The Origins of Alchemy in Graeco-Roman Egypt.* London: Frederick Muller Ltd.

MacCoull, L. S. B. (1988). 'Coptic Alchemy and Craft Technology in Early Islamic Egypt: The Papyrological Evidence'. In Marilyn J. Chiat, ed., *The Medieval Mediterranean.* Minneapolis: University of Minnesota Press, pp. 101–104.

Magee, Alexander Glenn. (2008). *Hegel and the Hermetic Tradition.* Ithaca: Cornel University Press.

al-Makkī, Abū Ṭālib Muḥammad. (2005). *Qūt al-Qulūb fī muʿāmalat al-maḥbūb wa waṣf ṭariq al-murīd ilā maqām al-tawḥīd*, vol. 1. Beirut: Dār al-kutub al-ʿilmiya.

Marlow Taylor, Gail (trans.). (2015). *The Alchemy of al-Razi: A Translation of the 'Book of Secrets'.* Scotts Valley: CreateSpace.

Martelli, Mateo. (2014). *The Four Books of Pseudo-Democritus.* London: Maney Publishing.

Martelli, Mateo. (2018). 'Translating Ancient Alchemy: Fragments of Graeco-Egyptian Alchemy in Arabic Compendia'. *Ambix*, 64, 1–17.

Martelli, Mateo and Rumor, Maddalena. (2014). *Near Eastern Origins of Graeco-Egyptian Alchemy*. Berlin: Max Planck Institute for the History of Science.

McLoughlin, Sean. 'Preliminary Notes on Ibn Arabi and Alchemy'. https://shorturl.at/uqYQK. Accessed online 9 June 2025.

Müller, Juliane. (2021). 'The Alchemical Symbols in the Manuscripts of "The Mirror of Wonders" (Mirāt al-'ajā'ib)'. *ASIA*, 75.2, 685–722.

Nagel, Thomas. (1974). 'What Is It Like to Be a Bat?'. *The Philosophical Review*, 83, 435–450.

Nasr, Seyyed Hossain (ed.). (2008). *Ismaili Thought in the Classical Age: From Jābir ibn Ḥayyān to Naṣīr al-Dīn Ṭūsī*. London: I.B. Tauris.

Newman, William. (2014). 'Mercury and Sulphur among the High Medieval Alchemists: From Rāzī and Avicenna to Albertus Magnus and Pseudo-Roger Bacon'. *Ambix*, 61, 327–344.

Newman, William. (2004). *Promethean Ambitions: Alchemy and the Quest to Perfect Nature*. Chicago: The University of Chicago Press.

Newman, William (ed.). (1991). *The Summa Perfectionis of Pseudo-Geber: A Critical Edition, Translation and Study*. Leiden: Brill.

Newman, William and Principe, Lawrence. (2002). Alchemy Tried in Fire. *Starkey, Boyle and the Fate of Helmontian Chymistry*. Chicago: The University of Chicago Press.

Norris, John. (2006). 'The Mineral Exaltations Theory of Metallogenesis in Pre-Modern Mineral Science'. *Ambix*, 53, 43–65.

Olsson, J. T. (2014). 'The World in the Arab Eyes'. *Bulletin of the School of Oriental and African Studies*, 77, 487–508.

Origen. (1953). *Contra Celsum*, translated by Henry Chadwick. Cambridge: Cambridge University Press.

Pan Ku. (1938). *The History of the Former Han Dynasty*, vol. 1, translated by H. Dubs. Baltimore: Waverly Press.

Paracelsus. (2007). *The Hermetic and Alchemical Writings*, translated by Arthur Edward White. London: Forgotten Books.

Pereira, Michela. (1999). 'Alchemy and the Use of Vernacular Languages in the Late Middle Ages'. *Speculum*, 74, 336–356.

Petrus Bonus. (1894). *The New Pearl of Great Price: A Treatise Concerning the Treasure and Most Precious Stone of the Philosophers*. London: James Elliott & Co.

Plato. (1925). 'Timaeus'. In *Plato in Twelve Volumes*, vol. 9, translated by W. R. M. Lamb. Cambridge, MA: Harvard University Press.

Plessner, M. (1954). 'Hermes Trismegistus and Arab Sciences'. *Studia Islamica*, 2, 45–59.

Plutarch. (1999). *Moralia V, with an English Translation by Frank Cole Babbitt*. Cambridge, MA: Harvard University Press.

Purkiss, Diane. (1996). *The Witch in History: Early Modern and Twentieth-Century Representations*. London: Routledge.

Qārī, Ibrahīm b. ʿAbd Allāh. (1959). *Manāqib Ibn ʿArabī*. Beirut: n.d.

al-Qazwīnī, ʾAbū Yaḥyā Zakariyyāʾ. (1960). *āthāt al-bilād wa akhbār al-ʿibād*. Beirut: Dāt al-Sāḍer.

al-Qazwīnī, ʾAbū Yaḥyā Zakariyyāʾ. (2006). *ʿAjāʾib al-makhlūqāt wa-gharāʾib al-mawjūdāt*. Cairo: Maktaba al-thaqāfa al-dīnīyya.

al-Raḥīlī, Abdallāh b. Ḍayf. (n.d.). *al-Akhlāq al-Fāḍila*. Riyad: Alsafeer Press.

Rajan, G. Raj. (1989). 'Religion and the Development of an Alchemical Philosophy of Transmutation in Ancient India'. In Z. R. W. M. von Martels, ed., Alchemy Revisited. Leiden: Brill, pp. 101–106.

Rašić, Dunja. (2026). *Azrael: Encounters with the Angel of Death in Islamicate Thought and Culture*. University Park: Penn State University Press.

Rašić, Dunja. (2024). *Bedeviled: Jinn Doppelgangers in Islam and Akbarian Sufism*. Albany: State University of New York Press.

Rašić, Dunja. (2022). 'Celestial Mechanics: Letters, Elements and Prime Matter in Ibn ʿArabī's Mystical Cosmogony'. *Journal of the Muhyiddin Ibn Arabi Society*, 72, 65–87.

Rašić, Dunja. (2023). 'Fāṭima, the Righteous Sorceress, and Ibn ʿArabī's Notions of Magic and Miracles'. *University of Pennsylvania Press Magic, Ritual, and Witchcraft*, 18, 364–381.

Rašić, Dunja. (2024). 'Masters of Dark Arts. Ibn ʿArabī's Records on African Sorcery, Qaḍīb al-Bān and the Power Known as Himma'. *Religions*, 15, 1–10.

Rašić, Dunja. (2025). *The Nightfolk: Ibn ʿArabī Behind the Veil of the Night*. Oakland: University of California Press.

Rašić, Dunja. (2023). 'Summoned Letters, Disjointed Letters and the Talisman of Ibn ʿArabī'. *Journal of Sufi Studies*, 13, 1–15.

Rašić, Dunja. (2021). *The Written World of God: The Cosmic Script and the Art of Ibn ʿArabī*. Oxford: Anqa Publishing.

Reeves, John. (2018). *Enoch from Antiquity to the Middle Ages*, vol. 1. Oxford: Oxford University Press.

Richter, Tonio Sebastian. (2015). 'The Master Spoke: "Take One of 'the Sun' and One Unit of Almulgam." Hitherto Unnoticed Coptic

Papyrological Evidence for Early Arabic Alchemy'. In Alexander T. Schubert, ed., *Documents and the History of the Early Islamic World*. Leiden: Brill, pp. 158–194.

Ritner, Robert. (1981). 'Hermes Pentamegistos'. *Gottinger Miszellen*, 49, 73–75.

Roberts, Alison. (2022). 'Rectifying the Pharaoh. Ibn ʿArabī, Dhū'l-Nūn and the Alchemy of Red Sulphur Part 1'. *Journal of Muhyiddin Ibn Arabi Society*, 71, 1–43.

Rosenthal, Franz. (1988). 'Ibn ʿArabī between "Philosophy" and "Mysticism": Sufism and Philosophy are Neighbors and Visit Each Other'. *Oriens*, 31, 1–35.

Ruska, Julius. (1926). *Tabula Smaragdina*. Heidelberg: Carl Winter's.

Ruspoli, Stéphane. (1964). *Le Livre des théophanies d'Ibn Arabî*. Damascus: Institut français de Damas.

Savage-Smith, Emilie (ed.). (2004). *Magic and Divination in Early Islam*. Burlington: Ashgate.

Schwartz-Salant, Nathan (ed.). (1994). *Jung on Alchemy*. London: Routledge.

Scott, Walter (trans.). (1924). *Hermetica*, vol. 1. Oxford: Clarendon Press.

Sedgwick, Mark. (2014). 'Ibn ʿArabi and the Contemporary West. Beshara and the Ibn 'Arabi Society'. *Islam and Christian–Muslim Relations*, 25, 389–390.

Sheppard, H. J. (1970). 'Alchemy: Origin or Origins?'. *Ambix*, 7, 69–84.

Shukin, Nicole. (2009). *Animal Capital: Rendering Life in Biopolitical Times*. Minneapolis: University of Minesota Press.

Smith, Pamela. (2017). *The Business of Alchemy: Science and Culture in the Holy Roman Empire*. New Jersey: Princeton University Press.

Sohn-Rethel, Alfred. (2021). *Intellectual and Manual Labor: A Critique of Epistemology*. Chicago: Haymarket Books.

Stapleton, H. E. (1949). 'The Sayings Attributed to Hermes Quoted in the Māʾ al-Waraqī of Ibn Umail'. *Ambix*, 3, 69–90.

Stapleton, H. E., and Lewis, G. L. (1962). 'Two Alchemical Treatises Attributed to Avicenna'. *Ambix*, 10, 41–82.

al-Subkī, Taqī al-Dīn. (1999). *Rafuʿ al-ḥājib mukhtaṣar Ibn al-Ḥājib*, vol. 4. Beirut: ʿālam al-kutub.

Taslimi, Manuchehr. (1954). 'An Examination of 'Nihāyat al-ṭalab' and the Determination of its Place and Value in the History of Islamic Chemistry', PhD diss., University of London.

Tertullian. (2018). *De cultu feminarum: The Complete Works of Tertullian*. Hastings: Delphi Classics.

al-Tha'ālabī, Abū Manṣūr 'Abd al-Malik. (n.d.). *Al-Latā'if wal-zarā'if.* Beirut: Dār al-manāhal.

Todd, Richard. (2014). *The Sufi Doctrine of Man. Ṣadr al-Dīn al-Qūnawī's Metaphysical Anthropology*. Leiden: Brill.

Tsing, Anna. (2021). *The Mushroom at the End of the World: On the Possibility of Life in Capitalist Ruins*. New Jersey: Princeton University Press.

Ulmann, Manfred. (1972). *Die Natur und Geheimwissenschaften im Islam*. Leiden: Brill.

Ulmann, Manfred. (1972). 'Kleopatra in einer arabischen alchemistischen Disputation'. *Wiener Zeitschrift für die Kinde des Morgenlandes*, 63/64, 158–176.

al-'Umarī, Faḍl Allāh. (2003). *Masālik al-abṣār fī mamālik al-amṣār*, vol. 22. Abu Dhabi: al-Majma' al-thaqāfī.

Van Bladel, Kevin. (2009). *The Arabic Hermes: From Pagan Safe to Prophet of Science*. Oxford: Oxford University Press.

Vialles, Noëlie. (1994). *Animals to Edible*. Cambridge: Cambridge University Press.

Von Uexküll, Jakob. (2010). *A Foray into the Worlds of Animals and Humans*. Minneapolis: University of Minnesota Press.

Wiedemann, Elihard. (1907). 'Zur Alchemie bei den Arabern'. *Journal für praktische Chemie*, 76, 65–123.

Winter, Jay. (ed.). (2015). *The Complete Book of Enoch*. Basel: Winter Publications.

Wittgenstein, Ludwig. (1994). *The Wittgenstein Reader*, edited by Anthony Kenny. Oxford: Blackwell.

Wolfe, Cary. (2009). *What Is Posthumanism?*. Minneapolis: University of Minnesota Press.

Yāqūt, Shihāb al-Dīn. (1997). *Mu'ajam al-buldān*, vol. 2. Beirut: Dār Ṣāder.

al-Zabīdī, Muḥammad b. Muḥammad. (2001). *Tāj al-arūs min jawāhir al-qāmūs*. Kuwait: Wizāra al-irshād wal-anbā'.

al-Zamakhsharī, Abū al-Qāsim Muḥammad. (1987). *Al-Mustaqṣā fī amthāl al-'arab*, vol. 1. Beirut: Dār al-kutub al-'ilmiya.

Zirnis, Peter. (1975). 'The Kitāb Ustuquss al-Uss of Jabir b. Ḥayyān', PhD diss., New York University.

Žižek, Slavoj. (2009). *The Sublime Object of Ideology*. Brooklyn: Verso Books.

Zosimos of Panopolis. (2011). *Muṣḥaf al-ṣuwar*, edited and translated by Theodor Abt and Salwa Fuad. Zurich: Living Human Heritage Publications.

Cambridge Elements

Magic

William Pooley
University of Bristol

William Pooley is Senior Lecturer in Modern History at the University of Bristol and co-editor of the forthcoming *Cambridge Companion to the Witch*. He is the author of *Body and Tradition in Nineteenth-century France: Félix Arnaudin and the Moorlands of Gascony* (2019) and co-author of the CUP Element *Creative Histories of Witchcraft: France, 1790–1940* (2022). His next book is a history of witchcraft in France from the French Revolution to World War Two.

About the Series

Elements in Magic aims to restore the study of magic, broadly defined, to a central place within culture: one which it occupied for many centuries before being set apart by changing discourses of rationality and meaning. Understood as a continuing and potent force within global civilisation, magical thinking is imaginatively approached here as a cluster of activities, attitudes, beliefs and motivations which include topics such as alchemy, astrology, divination, exorcism, the fantastical, folklore, haunting, supernatural creatures, necromancy, ritual, spirit possession and witchcraft.

Cambridge Elements

Magic

Elements in the Series

'Ritual Litter' Redressed
Ceri Houlbrook

Representing Magic in Modern Ireland: Belief, History, Culture
Andrew Sneddon

Creative Histories of Witchcraft: France, 1790–1940
Poppy Corbett, Anna Kisby Compton and William G. Pooley

Witchcraft and Paganism in Midcentury Women's Detective Fiction
Jem Bloomfield

The Gut: A Black Atlantic Alimentary Tract
Elizabeth Pérez

The Donkey King: Asinine Symbology in Ancient and Medieval Magic
Emily Selove

Amulets in Magical Practice
Jay Johnston

Staging Witchcraft before the Law: Skepticism, Performance as Proof, and Law as Magic in Early Modern Witch Trials
Julie Stone Peters

Lowcountry Conjure Magic: Historical Archaeology on a Plantation Slave Quarter
Sharon K. Moses

Gerald Gardner and the Creation of Wicca
John Callow

Conjuring the Arab Magician: Intercultural Histories of Magic
Gal Sofer

The Elixir: A Posthumanist Approach to Alchemy in Akbarian Sufism and Islam
Dunja Rašić

A full series listing is available at: www.cambridge.org/EMGI

For EU product safety concerns, contact us at Calle de José Abascal, 56–1°,
28003 Madrid, Spain or eugpsr@cambridge.org.

www.ingramcontent.com/pod-product-compliance
Lightning Source LLC
LaVergne TN
LVHW011855060526
838200LV00054B/4352
* 9 7 8 1 0 0 9 7 7 7 0 1 8 *

www.ingramcontent.com/pod-product-compliance
Lightning Source LLC
LaVergne TN
LVHW072022060526
838200LV00009B/231
* 9 7 8 1 7 7 8 9 2 0 5 5 4 *